Artist Paul Kane reaches Fort Vancouver after sketch-tour through West.

1847

Telegraph line between Toronto and Quebec City completed.

Toronto Society of Arts founded.

> RAILROADS, &c.
>
> **Montreal & Lachine Railroad**
>
> FALL ARRANGEMENT.
>
> ON and after THIS DAY until further NO-TICE, Trains will leave at the undermentioned hours (Sundays excepted.)
>
> | FROM MONTREAL. | FROM LACHINE. | |
> |---|---|---|
> | 7¼ A.M. | 8¼ A.M. | Or on the arrival of the Steamer which may be due and in sight. |
> | 11½ A.M. | 12 M. | |
> | 3 P.M. | 3½ P.M. | |
> | 4½ P.M. | 5 P.M. | |
> | 6 P.M. | 6½ P.M. | |
> | 7 A.M. | 7¼ A.M. | |
>
> ON SUNDAYS.
>
> | FROM MONTREAL. | FROM LACHINE. |
> |---|---|
> | 10¼ A.M. | 11 A.M. |
> | 3 P.M. | On arrival of Steamer. |
> | 7 do | Do do |
>
> Freight carried at very low rates
>
> JNO. FARROW, Supt. & Treas.
>
> Montreal, Sept. 17, 1850. 172

First railway completed between Montreal and Lachine.

Reform Party led by Robert Baldwin and Louis LaFontaine sweeps elections in Canada West and Canada East.

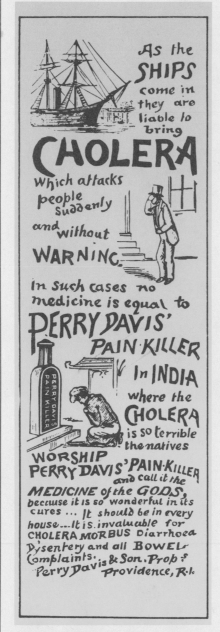

As the SHIPS come in they are liable to bring CHOLERA which attacks people suddenly and without WARNING. In such cases no medicine is equal to PERRY DAVIS' PAIN-KILLER In INDIA where the CHOLERA is so terrible the natives WORSHIP PERRY DAVIS' PAIN-KILLER and call it the MEDICINE of the GODS, because it is so wonderful in its cures ... It should be in every house...It is invaluable for CHOLERA MORBUS Diarrhoea Dysentery and all BOWEL Complaints. Perry Davis & Son, Props Providence, R.I.

Approximately 10,000 immigrants die in typhus and cholera epidemics.

Alexander Murray builds Fort Yukon for HBC in Russian-owned Alaska.

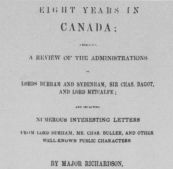

EIGHT YEARS IN CANADA: ... A REVIEW OF THE ADMINISTRATIONS ... LORDS DURHAM AND SYDENHAM, SIR CHAS. BAGOT, AND LORD METCALFE; ... NUMEROUS INTERESTING LETTERS FROM LORD DURHAM, MR. CHAS. BULLER, AND OTHER WELL-KNOWN PUBLIC CHARACTERS ... BY MAJOR RICHARDSON,

John Richardson p[ublishes?] Years in Canada, a[...] governors.

1848 DISCARD

Paul Kane's first exhibition of paintings opens in Toronto.

Nova Scotia and New Brunswick granted responsible government.

Niagara Falls runs dry due to ice jams on river.

> £20,000 **REWARD** WILL BE GIVEN BY Her Majesty's Government TO ANY PARTY OR PARTIES, OF ANY COUNTRY, WHO SHALL RENDER EFFICIENT ASSISTANCE TO THE CREWS OF THE **DISCOVERY SHIPS** UNDER THE COMMAND OF **SIR JOHN FRANKLIN,**
>
> 1.—To any Party or Parties who, in the judgment of the Board of Admiralty, shall discover and effectually relieve any of the Crews of Her Majesty's Ships "Erebus" and "Terror," the Sum of **£20,000.**
>
> 2.—To any Party or Parties who, in the judgment of the Board of Admiralty, shall discover and effectually relieve any of the Crews of Her Majesty's Ships "Erebus" and "Terror," or shall convey such intelligence as shall lead to the relief of such Crews or any of them, the Sum of **£10,000.**
>
> 3.—To any Party or Parties who, in the judgment of the Board of Admiralty, shall by virtue of his or their efforts first succeed in ascertaining their fate, **£10,000.**
>
> W. A. B. HAMILTON, Secretary of the Admiralty.

Three expeditions comb the Arctic in search of John Franklin.

Hamilton *Spectator* begins publication

1849

First Intercolonial Confe[rence] held at Halifax.

Telegraph connection co[mpleted] between Halifax and Sai[nt John] links Maritimes with U.S.

[PUNCH IN CANADA]

PUBLIC ARCHIVES OF CANADA

Punch in Canada begins publication.

Parliament building in Montreal destroyed by fire by rioters protesting Rebellion Losses Bill.

Vancouver Island becomes a Crown colony.

Annexation Manifesto for union with U.S. signed by 325 Montrealers, from John Molson to Louis-Joseph Papineau.

Date Due

Pioneer Days

Robert Whale's View of Hamilton *(1853) from the mountain shows a few pioneer log cabins on the outskirts of the booming city and railway depot.*

Previous page: *Bible in hand, a Methodist circuit-riding evangelist preaches a fiery sermon at a rural camp-meeting. A "love feast" followed the service.*

Joy Carroll
Pioneer Days
1840/1860

Canada's Illustrated Heritage

Canada's Illustrated Heritage

Publisher: Jack McClelland
Editorial Consultant: Pierre Berton
Historical Consultant: Michael Bliss
Editor-in-Chief: Toivo Kiil
Associate Editors: Michael Clugston
Clare McKeon
Harold Quinn
Jean Stinson
Assistant Editor: Marta Howard
Design: William Hindle
Lynn Campbell
Neil Fraser Cochrane
Cover Artist: Alan Daniel
Picture Research: Lembi Buchanan
Michel Doyon
Betty Gibson
Christine Jensen
Margot Sainsbury

ISBN: 0-9196-4417-1

N.S.L. Natural Science of Canada Limited
254 Bartley Drive
Toronto, Ontario M4A 1G1

Printed and bound in Canada

*Card games, chess checkers, backgammon and billiards were popular evening and rainy-day
diversions in men's clubs and most homes. Whist, picquet, quadrille (all variations of the
modern game of bridge), vingt-et-un (twenty-one) and cribbage were after-dinner drawing-room
games, sometimes played with colourful decks. Poker, introduced from the U.S. in the mid-1800s,
was strictly a man's game, often played for high stakes and roundly condemned by some churches.*

The 1850s saw hundreds of miles of track laid between towns from Sarnia to Rivière du Loup. However, with frequent breakdowns and delays, passengers (like this family picknicking at Toronto's Union Station in 1859) were wise not to bet on reaching their destination for the next meal.

6

What Did the Simple Folk Do?

There is a way of doin' everything, if you only know how to go about it.

Thomas Haliburton, *Sam Slick's Wise Saws,* 1853

There was no *nation*, of course, only a scattering of half-connected settlements optimistically called "provinces" by ambitious politicians. In the decades between 1840 and 1860, a tremulous, shared parliament glued Canada East to Canada West. In the vast virgin acres of British North America beyond the frontier of the Red River colony, Hudson's Bay Company factors ruled sprawling domains with iron hearts and all the trappings of feudal lords. And on the outer edge, Victoria, still a fort but soon to be a stodgy settlement, clung desperately to the Crown, for fear of being swept into the American banquet.

The haughty Arctic was forced to yield a few of her chilling secrets – the Northwest Passage for one, during the dogged search for a missing adventurer, John Franklin. The Maritimes scrambled for fish, timber and territory in bruising competition with the United States and the blustering state of Maine to the south. And, as always, Newfoundland stood alone.

During the twenty-year span from 1840 to 1860, railroads first began to rumble over the landscape, rioters wrecked the parliament buildings in Montreal, and New Brunswick entrepreneur Joseph Cunard bankrupted the lumbertown of Chatham when his creditors came to call. While James Douglas ruled the Pacific Coast from a crude fort on Vancouver Island, Joseph Howe was fighting for a rail link between Halifax and Quebec City. John Palliser, Irish gentleman hunter, was hiking across the West wrestling bears and surveying the grasslands, and tough Bishop John Strachan was doing his damnedest in Toronto to secure the promised land – those elusive Clergy Reserves handed to the Church of England in an earlier time. Roman Catholic bishops, ever mindful of the priceless perks of separate schools, were juggling their flocks with seemingly folded hands. Orangemen, marching each July 12 in memory of King Billy, managed to wrangle with local Catholics at the same time.

As for culture, a little bit went a long way: among the offerings were William Henry Bartlett's refining of rough eastern architecture, Paul Kane's etchings of the Indians' plight, Catherine Parr Traill and her sister Susanna Moodie recalling their lives in the *Literary Garland*, and William Kirby producing the *United Empire Loyalists*, an epic poem recounting more than anybody had ever cared to know about Loyalist migration to the Niagara Peninsula.

Politically it was a time when British governors – a string of them – still tried to manage the affairs of state for French and English Canadians; a time of strong opinions and eloquent speech-making; a

CHECK GATE !

BELLEVILLE & FRANKFORD ROAD.

RATE OF TOLLS.

For every Vehicle loaded or otherwise, drawn by two horses or other beasts. - - - - - 1 d.

For each additional horse or other beast. - 1d.

For every Vehicle drawn by one horse or other beast. 1d.

For every Horse with or without rider. - - 1d.

For every head of Neat Cattle. - - - - d.

FOR EVERY SCORE OR LESS OF SHEEP OR SWINE 1D

TOLLS TO BE PAID AT EACH TIME OF PASSING

Farmers bringing their produce to market, or going to town to shop or pick up mail, had to pay for each mile of the way. Toll gates built every four or five miles exacted fees for every vehicle, man and beast, supposedly to pay the cost of maintenance. Usually the money was pocketed by the road-building company and the road left in poor repair. Small wonder that farmers delighted in "running the gate."

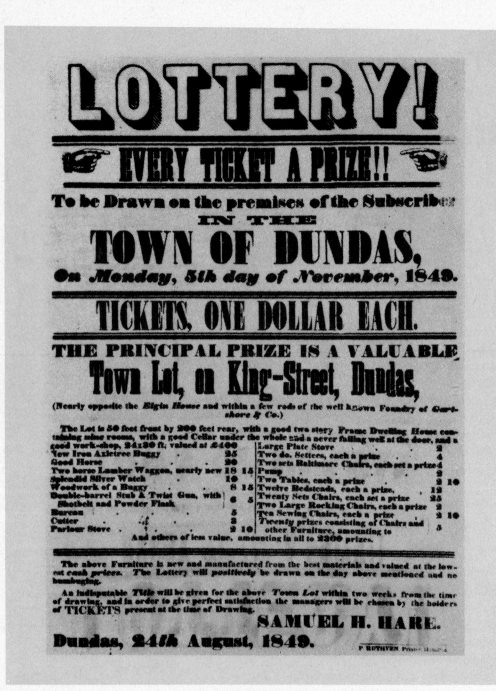

EVERY TICKET A PRIZE!! *(sound familiar?)* at the Dundas Lottery. Top prize: a two-storey *frame house, with buggy, horse, silver watch, shot-gun, furniture and odds-and sods to the* *runners-up. No humbuging, either. Tickets a dollar each. Total value of goods: £700.*

time of shady railway deals and vote-buying; and a time that saw the emergence of such legendary leaders as Louis Hippolyte LaFontaine, Joe Howe, George-Etienne Cartier, and a young lawyer from Kingston named John Alexander Macdonald.

And what did the simple folk do? They breathed clean air while constantly struggling to support life. For them it was slogging in killing wilderness isolation, risking their lives for the right to vote.

Every facet of life was appallingly difficult for a working man. He travelled through the desolate country by canoe, horse or on foot – or he stayed home. Only a few could afford the luxury of passage on a lake boat, stage coach or a seat on the new-fangled railroad. Every day, in every way, he fought harder and harder just to survive – always in fear of crop failure, economic depression and immigrants carrying cholera, small pox and typhus on their ragged clothing. Women died with alarming frequency in childbirth. Letters home to relatives in England, Ireland and Scotland often contained the reassuring phrase, "we are all still alive" – unless, of course, some unfortunate had died since the last post.

a do-it–yourself age

It was still very much a do-it-yourself age. Men shod their own horses, built their own houses and brewed their own beer. Women cured meat, tanned hides, wove cloth and mined salt from prairie lakes. Voyageurs paddled heavy *bateaux* along swift rivers and trappers snowshoed for endless miles to gather furs. Sailors lived on salt meat and cereal, their gums often sagging with scurvy.

But there was plenty of opportunity to make a fortune or just a good living, if a man had the courage. Crown land was either cheap or free. During the semi-annual migrations the skies were still clouded with game birds and the woods were thick with deer, elk, and moose. Out on the prairies there were still herds of buffalo. Streams, in most places at least, were packed with trout, salmon or pike—the woods dotted with berries.

bothersome news

At mid-century, however, the members of the New Brunswick legislature received some bothersome news. Mill dams were obstructing spawning salmon and sawdust was choking the trout. Would it be more advantageous to stop the saw mills and lose those jobs or destroy river fisheries? The answer was a question as well. When there were so many rivers, so many trees, so many fish, surely a little sawdust couldn't do that much harm?

Life moved forward despite such trivial considerations. In parliament, the representatives of the two Canadas passed far-reaching legislation: the railway Guarantee Act giving much-needed government support to budding railroads; the Municipal Corporations Act to oil the machinery of local rule; a revamped education system for the working classes; a regular mail service by steamship across the Atlantic, telegraph lines to major cities; settled boundaries between the United States and Canada; a postal rate within reach of the average pocketbook.

The world was growing smaller, tightening with improved communications, and once the Grand Trunk Railroad gathered steam, there was no telling what might happen. Even the western spaces might be tamed, making the new colony of British Columbia a plausible candidate for a broad confederacy.

By the time 1860 touched the calendar, people were hopeful, seeing clearly for the first time the possibility of *one country* as reality instead of dream. Canada just might stretch from sea to sea.

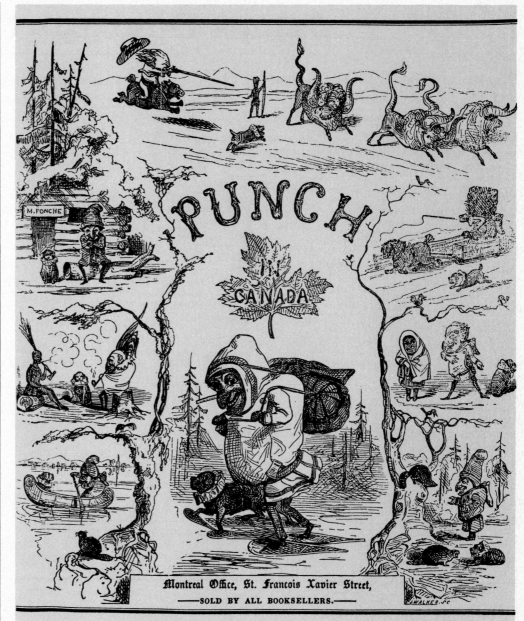

Offspring of the English humour magazine (founded in 1841), Punch in Canada made its debut eight years later—the first publication to take a satirical poke at the "sacred cows" ruminating in the pastures of Canadian politics, high-society and business.

James Duncan's Canada

James Duncan's Canada was Montreal—the city, its environs and especially its people. Born in Ireland in 1806, he came to Canada at age nineteen, taught drawing at young ladies' academies, ran a commercial design house, and occasionally saw his work in print in *Illustrated London News*. Mornings would find him on street corners, pencil in hand, sketching beggars and businessmen, pedlars and society ladies (dressed *à la Parisienne*), doing their rounds. At nights, he and his artist friend Cornelius Krieghoff may have quaffed a pint at Widow Barton's, comparing sketches of town and rural life.

Looking west along Montreal's main commercial avenue, Rue Notre-Dame, in 1850, Nelson's Monument and church spires tower above the bustle of afternoon traffic. One weary shopper has plopped himself down on the sidewalk to watch the world go by. Two others are holding up the wall surrounding the Court House.

With winter freeze-up, the tall masts of windships and smokestacks of steamers vanished from Montreal's harbour, replaced by dozens of ice-cutters' huts.
Wielding ice ploughs and long-toothed saws, workers cut two-by-four foot slabs, hoisted them onto sleighs and stored them in warehouses for next summer's use.

11

Charles Dickens, the English novelist, visited Canada in 1842, and spent the month of May living at Rasco's Hotel near the Montreal waterfront. His daily stroll often took him to the quay, where he observed immigrants "grouped in hundreds on the public wharfs about their chests and boxes".

CHAPTER ONE

Tragedy at Grosse Isle

Many of the emigrants have slept all night in the open air on the damp ground, with no other covering except their wearing apparel. We found patients suffering from fever and dysentry in this destitute and neglected condition....

Papers Relative to Emigration, December 20, 1847

Viewed from a ship at anchor on the St. Lawrence River, Grosse Isle was paradise found. It shimmered seductively thirty miles down river from Quebec City, a jewel three miles long and one mile wide; firred, willowed and as green as Ireland herself.

Robert Whyte, a cabin passenger on one of the 224 ships sailing out of Irish ports for Canada in 1847, described Grosse Isle in his diary:

At the far end were rows of white tents and marquees, resembling the encampment of an army; somewhat nearer was the little fort and residence of the superintendent physician, and nearer still the chapel, seamen's hospital and little village with its wharf and few sail boats; the most adjacent extremity being rugged rocks among which grew beautiful fir trees.

Surely this small island was a taste of the prize fifty thousand Irish peasants had imagined all through a cruel trans-Atlantic voyage. Unfortunately it was only an illusion. Grosse Isle was the

nation's quarantine station, and that summer ship's fever (typhus) raged on the tattered armada of emigrant vessels awaiting medical clearance. Passengers who could manage to stand on deck were reminded of this ugly truth by the rude and constant removal of their dead.

While the island beckoned enticingly just out of reach, corpses, covered with filth and bedsores and more often than not wearing only a few rags, were carried up a narrow ladder from each ship's hold. On deck, a rope was tied around the bodies and they were hoisted with "head and naked limbs dangling for a moment in mid-air" before being lowered unceremoniously into a waiting row boat. They were then dumped upon the rocky shore to await burial.

In the beginning rough coffins were provided, but when the death rate soared, grave-diggers settled for trenches and stacked the dead in them like cordwood. Six men worked constantly every day at the island cemetery. As the temperature rose in the summer sun, a horde of rats scampered down the ships' guys and came ashore. They dug through the shallow covering on the graves and began to gnaw on the decaying human flesh. Grave-diggers poured hundreds of cartloads of earth over the trenches to prevent rats from dragging off limbs. It was just one more grotesque episode in an unrelenting nightmare.

Most emigrants had been tenants on large Irish

"In this secluded spot lie the mortal remains of 5,424 persons who flying from Pestilence and Famine in Ireland in the year 1847 found in America but a Grave."

There were no chaises longues or deck chairs aboard the Day Spring when this missionary and his family sailed from Halifax for New Zealand in 1860. The journey took over three months.

estates. The blighted potato crop of 1845, followed by another disastrous harvest in 1846, brought famine and fever to the whole country. The potato was the staple of the national diet. By 1847, English landlords plagued with destitute and starving tenants, were eager to ship them to the New World. It was the ultimate solution and skirted land reform while consolidating holdings.

rotting wooden tubs

Emigrants were crammed into any ship that would sail, many of them rotting wooden tubs once used to transport lumber. There was no accommodation for separation of the sexes, nor cooking, washing or toilet facilities. Nobody seemed to realize that the passengers were stricken with typhus and would carry the lethal disease with them to North America.

Once aboard, fever patients were wedged in narrow bunks with the healthy, their ravings and incontinence preventing sleep by night and making life by day utterly unbearable. The dead were left lying with the living because no one wanted to carry bodies up on deck. The afflicted were often left without food, water or medicine unless some caring neighbour doled out a few necessities. Beds were "teaming with abominations" and straw mattresses were seldom, if ever, aired.

Stephen De Vere, a member of a wealthy family from County Limerick, decided to travel steerage that year in order to observe for himself the plight of the fleeing Irish peasants.

Before the emigrant has been at sea a week, he is an altered man. How can it be otherwise? Hundreds of people, men, women, and children of all ages, from the drivelling idiot of 90 to the babe just born, all huddled together, without light, without air, wallowing in filth and breathing the fetid atmosphere.

Life on *all* Irish emigrant ships was miserable

beyond imagination. In 1847 alone, 54,462 passengers sailed from Ireland for the Province of Canada and almost all were penniless, hungry and dressed in lice-infested rags. Twenty-five thousand died – at sea, at the quarantine station itself or as they later painfully made their way to farms and towns in the interior.

Typhus was prevalent at the time in army camps, city slums and ships. The mortality rate was always around fifty percent. The disease began with a high fever (105 degrees F was common), inability to move, severe headaches, intense delirium and body rash usually accompanied by dysentery. The tongues of victims were covered by a whitish fur; in severe cases the tongue became black and rolled up like a ball in the back of the mouth. Bluish spots appeared all over the body – the extent of the eruption indicating the severity of the attack. The second stage was coma, the patient's eyes wide-open but unseeing. Death occurred either from toxaemia (blood poisoning) or from the high fever itself.

fouled beds and garbage

Ships reaching Grosse Isle in mid-summer plied a river filthy with floating straw from fouled beds, garbage and barrels containing "the vilest matter" left by earlier arrivals as they cleaned out the ships holds. Those passengers designated "healthy" were taken off by small steamers for the ports of Quebec City, Montreal, or in some cases, were taken directly ashore to Grosse Isle where they were quarantined. The sick were destined for the fever sheds.

The term "healthy" was always questionable. Father O'Reilly, one of the Catholic priests who braved Grosse Isle that awful summer, visited the "healthy" in tents on the eastern end of the island and gave the last rites to fifty of them. The Right Reverend George Jehoshaphat Mountain, Angli-

Epidemics of typhus and cholera raged through Quebec and Montreal in the '40s and '50s. Working in fetid immigration sheds, many "sisters of mercy" fell prey to the diseases.

The Misadventures of the Emigrant

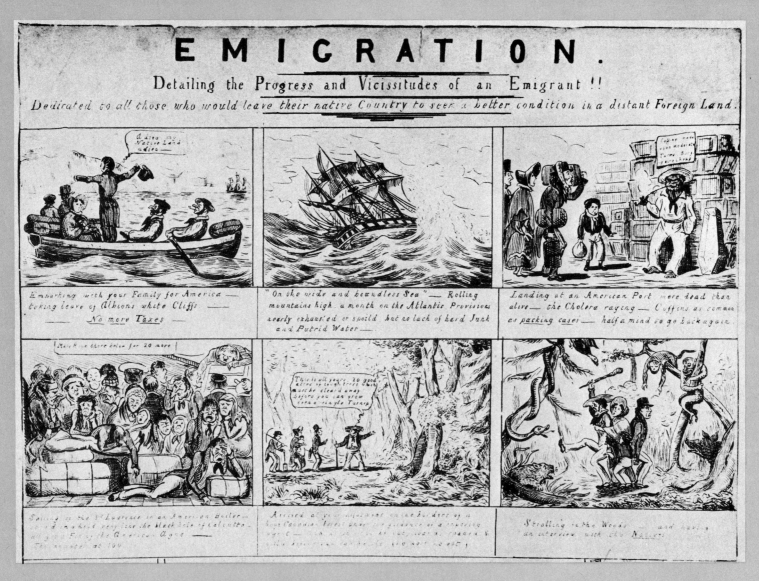

Oh, the trials of the naive and luckless emigrant! (1) Embarking with your Family for America – taking leave of Albion's white Cliffs – No more Taxes (2) "On the wide and boundless Sea" – Rolling mountains high, a month on the Atlantic. Provisions nearly exhausted or spoild, but no lack of hard Junk and Putrid Water (3) Landing at an American Port, more dead than alive – the Cholera raging – Coffins as common as packing cases – half a mind to go back again (4) Sailing up the St Laurence in an American Boiler – stored in a hold very like the black hole of Calcutta – all got a Fit of the American Ague – thermometer at 100 (5) Arrived at your allotment on the borders of a high Canadian Forest under the guidance of a imposing agent – every stick of it is cut, cleared, spaded & tilled before you can settle (No work, no eat) (6) Strolling in the Woods – and having an interview with the Natives.

(7) A view of your Hut — digging under a hot July Sun — thermometer at 90 in the shade — infested by Musquitoes with stings like stocking needles (8) In exploring the neighboring land, you tumble over an Alligator — makes him run — the devil catch the hindmost! (9) Visited by a Settler — not the Tax gatherer (10) . . . a Spider as big as a crabb spins a web on your hat & a Scorpion creeps into your Hut unobserved, takes a lodging under the bed & gives birth to a numerous brood (11) Sleeping under Buffalo skins lined with fleas as big as blue bottles — alarmed in the night by a colony of Rats in your room . . . (12) . . . Visited by a neighbor the nearest by 5 miles, who sees no reason why you a small Farmer with a large family should not be like him in about 12 or 14 years . . . (13) Hut on Fire yet a 3rd time . . . sits down unable to do anything . . . (14) Fall into the hands of Cannibals — you & your family's lives at stake — being roasted for a Feast yourself escapes by a miracle (15) The Finale or wind up — Poor, Friendless & Broken down — like Robinson Crusoe on an uninhabited Island — looking out for a Ship to convey you back to Old England — works your passage back & land sans Money, sans Friends & sans everything!!!

can Bishop of Quebec, saw people on shore screaming for water; patients lying on the bare ground in tents awash with rain; children covered with vermin. He reported seeing the body of an emaciated young boy who, while walking along with other emigrants, sat down under a tree to rest – and quietly died.

Grosse Isle had first been declared a quarantine station during the cholera epidemic of 1832. Early in 1847, Dr. George M. Douglas, medical officer in charge, became alarmed. Like others, he knew from reading the newspapers that a great famine was sweeping Ireland. A vast emigration was bound to hit the shores of North America, he reasoned, as soon as spring sailing began. Douglas asked the government of the Province of Canada for £3,000 to increase his staff and facilities. But nobody in power was listening. He was allotted a meagre £300, a small steamer to carry the healthy to Quebec City, and told to purchase a sailing vessel if he could find one for £50, presumably to carry supplies. Somehow he managed to add fifty beds to his hospital, bringing accommodation close to two hundred.

an isle of chaos

When the ice cleared from the St. Lawrence late that spring, one of the first arrivals, the *Syria*, brought eighty-four cases of typhus with her. Within four days, eight more ships had raised the total number of afflicted to 430. Already the island hospital was dangerously overcrowded and the sick were put in old passenger sheds (meant only as temporary shelter) and in army tents. But ships continued to anchor and conditions on the little island became more and more chaotic. On May 26, thirty vessels (with ten thousand people aboard) awaited clearance. By May 29, there were thirty-six ships in the harbour and by the middle of July the line extended two miles down river.

New sheds were thrown up quickly – but without privies. The surrounding bushes became a mess. There was no ventilation, no sanitation and the stench was overpowering. Beds were built in double tiers. Those lying on the lower bunks suffered abominably from the drip of excrement leaking through the boards above them. Often the sick were left on wooden slats on the ground. When straw or mattresses were used, they were never changed from one patient to the next.

Medical aid was almost non-existent despite the best efforts of Douglas. "Medical men were disgusted with the disagreeable nature of their duties in treating such filthy cases," he reported. (When the harbour closed for the season in October, four doctors had died along with eighteen medical assistants. On a single day, twelve of the fourteen medical staff were ill).

High pay failed to lure nurses to the island. Little wonder. They were given beds in the same stinking sheds as the sick, had no privacy in which to change their clothes and were expected to eat their meals – the same dreary food given to patients – in the fever sheds. The chances of nurses catching typhus under these conditions were almost one hundred percent. They had every right to inquire who would care for *them* if they fell sick.

In sheer desperation the inmates of the common jail in Quebec City were ordered to help with the typhus victims on Grosse Isle. Robbing the dead soon became a favourite pastime. Compounding the difficulties of Douglas and his staff, police sent to Grosse Isle from Quebec City to maintain order were prone to drunkenness and immorality.

Medical knowledge was still primitive. Typhus is now known to be caused by the bites of infected body lice or fleas, but at the time of the Grosse Isle epidemic this was not understood. Unsanitary conditions fostered the spread of disease. Thirty-seven cases of smallpox appeared amidst the misery, not totally unexpectedly. Though Edward Jenner developed a vaccine in the late 18th century, it was not made compulsory in the British Isles until 1853.

Conditions at Grosse Isle were so out of control by July that Douglas was instructed by his superiors in government to let the "healthy" go on to Quebec City or Montreal without the two-week period of quarantine. A medical officer would board ship, order a deck parade of all those able to walk, and inspect their tongues for dryness and the whitish fuzz associated with typhus. If passed, emigrants were then crammed aboard small steamers and exposed to the cold night air and burning sun. Many were already coming down with fever, and according to some official estimates, more than half the passengers of any single boatload arriving at Montreal wharves were near death.

As early as June 8, Douglas had warned authorities in both cities that they could expect an epidemic. "Good God!" he exclaimed, "What evils will befall the city whenever they alight."

He was right. Typhus epidemics occurred in both places. Quebec City took steps quickly to hospitalize those landing. Fever sheds were erected at St. Roch near the Marine Hospital, and the governor-general arranged for a wing of the cavalry barracks on the Plains of Abraham to be used as a temporary hospital.

But a severe outbreak could not be prevented in the poorer lodging houses of Lower Town. Yet on September 10, the Quebec Board of Health was dissolved because the situation was no longer considered dangerous.

In Montreal, things were even bleaker. Being the commercial centre of the Canadas, it drew more emigrants. Thousands of old, sick and destitute Irish were left on the waterfront with no idea where to go or how to get there. The Montreal Board of Health was formed on June 5 to cope with this new emergency. Cheap boarding houses

The shifty herb doctor, carrying his bundle of roots, plants, berries and flower petals, was a common hawker on the streets and in the market place. Pharmacy as we know it was in its infancy, and even hospitals had their own herb gardens, from which were prepared the plasters, poultices, ointments and extracts used in the treatment of diseases from cholera to croup.

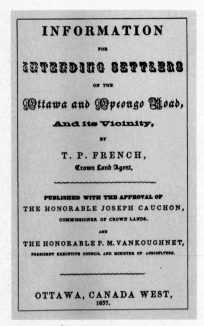

*Settlers in the Ottawa Valley
followed close on the heels of
French and Irish lumberjacks,
supplying the camps and shanty-
towns with farm produce. Feuds
were common, however, prompted
by farmers charging outrageous
prices for their goods, or the
petulant Irish "Shiners" trying
to drive the French bûcherons
from prime lumbering territories.*

were closed and plans drawn up to hospitalize the sick near Windmill Point above the Lachine Canal. Before these edicts could take effect, hundreds of bewildered emigrants lay on the wharves and crowded the receiving sheds. While harbour authorities forbade the landing of any more refugees, a few unscrupulous captains managed to unload their cargo.

Ordinary, normally God-fearing citizens of Montreal took to a new sport. It became chic to stroll down to the docks in the late afternoon and stare at the dying while they frantically pleaded for food, water – help of *any* kind. It was a macabre human zoo; a whiff of the Roman circus.

Many responsible citizens were outraged that the city could be invaded by a plague. On July 10, a general meeting was held in Bonsecours Market to demand that the infected newcomers be moved to Boucherville Island. Medical consultants pointed out that this was impractical: it would just create another Grosse Isle, where all supplies would have to be shipped in with great difficulty. The popular mayor of Montreal, John Mills, gave a pragmatic but rather chilling speech pointing out that the danger of refuse from victims being carried down river to Montreal was small because the "drainings of the whole city of Montreal" already emptied into the St. Lawrence through a creek above the city's water intake pipe. He reasoned that if the people could survive the filth produced by the fifty thousand inhabitants of the city, a few more sick immigrants could hardly increase the evil. (Mills died in the autumn of that year of typhus contracted when working among the fever victims).

By August, emigrants were taken to the hospital at Point St. Charles if they were ill, and if they appeared well, to open sheds on the river bank. Barges, grossly overcrowded, then transported them to Kingston or Toronto.

It came as no surprise to the informed that Toronto reported 872 fever patients on August 15. Irish peasants roamed about the farmland of Canada West seeking work, shelter, food – but settlers were reluctant to take them in. Stephen De Vere reported that during a tour that summer he met destitute Irish everywhere he went. Families were often separated and De Vere wrote:

Travelling from Prescott to Bytown, by stage, I saw a poor woman with an infant in her arms and a child pulling at her skirt, crying as they went along. The driver compassionately took them up and the way-farer wept her thanks. She had lost her husband upon the voyage and was going to Bytown to her brother who had come out the previous year, and having made some money by lumbering in the woods, remitted to her the means of joining him.

This story ended more happily than most as the woman found her brother in Bytown.

When the last vessel arrived in the St. Lawrence in early November, Grosse Isle had closed for the season. But the arrival of the *Richard Watson* out of Sligo, carrying 165 passengers from the Irish estates of Lord Palmerston, was an exclamation mark to the whole summer. According to Health Officer Dr. Joseph Parent of Quebec City, this was the poorest group of all. They arrived wearing rags, without shoes or stockings, the children completely naked and shivering in the cold. One young woman, he noted sadly, wore only the canvas of a biscuit-bag.

And so the survivors of the plague spread throughout Canada East and Canada West, trying desperately to build a new life for themselves, against hostility and without resources. Many remained in Montreal to form a ghetto known as Griffintown; some found their way to Bytown; others went to Kingston, Prescott, Toronto, Guelph and London. Thousands more found their way to the United States where they hoped for a warmer welcome and more hopeful future.

Market Place

William Raphael, a German-born Jewish artist who emigrated to Montreal in 1857, captured the activity of Montreal's waterfront as only an immigrant could. Behind Bonsecours Market, a fiddler is sawing out a folk-tune for his audience of children, pipe-smoking vendors and an old, foot-tapping habitant. *Two women sit in the shadows (left) gossiping, while a well-dressed gent sporting a walking-stick and showing off his gold watch chain flirts with a couple of ladies (right). There are hints of Montreal's changing population, too. An immigrant with a long, curved pipe waits patiently while the pawn-broker and a woman customer (centre) finish haggling. It looks as though he is about to hock a few precious heirlooms brought along from Europe. It is early autumn, still warm enough for boys to go barefoot, but in three months the river will freeze, the pedlars will move inside and prices will go up.*

Dining à la Carte

Oysters the size of a man's hand, lobsters as large as barnyard chickens, fresh and saltwater fish stretching across the dining room table, pheasants and partridges big as turkeys, mountainous cakes, puddings and jellies – those who could afford it ate very well (and probably far too much) in mid-19th century Canada. "Three copious meals, often of twelve or fourteen dishes each, are daily served up," noted N. P. Willis, a visitor in 1842. Most meat was eaten boiled, broiled or roasted. Wild game and fowl were considered delicacies, since raised livestock was often tough or gamey. And desserts? Don't count the calories, just enjoy, and wash it down with champagne.

Lobsters, oysters, scallops and salmon were shipped in barrels or pack-ice from the Maritimes to Canada (13,000 cases from one Miramichi village alone in 1845).

Hotels and dining rooms like Copain's, especially in Montreal and Quebec City, were noted for their wide range of imported wines.

Plate V.

Plate VII.

"Made dishes" of meat or fish covered with sauce become popular around the mid-1800s. During the depression a little had to go a long way even with food.

Solomon's Temple, Jenny Lind Cake and Plum Pudding (45 eggs, 4 cups of brandy, 5 qts. of raisins, etc.) or Black Prune Cake (for funerals) were sweet delights.

23

Horrors and disasters seem to have held a special fascination for Quebec artist Joseph Légaré: the total eclipse of 1830; the colera epidemic of 1834; the Cape Diamond rock slide of 1841; the fires in Saint-Jean (above) and Saint-Roch in 1845; and the burning of Parliament in 1849.

CHAPTER TWO

Is Parliament Burning?

You call yourself a Rouge. There may have been at one time a reddish tinge about you, but I could observe it becoming by degrees fainter. Seriously, you would make a decent Conservative, if you gave your own judgement a fair chance, and cut loose from . . . those other beggars.

John A. Macdonald to A. T. Galt, November 2, 1857

He looked like Napoleon. His high, polished forehead was adorned with a single dark kiss-curl, his jowl ponderous, his eyes inflamed with *cause* and his manner consistently showy. He wore the essence of leadership like strong perfume – when he beckoned, men followed.

As he tramped determinedly through the chill April air at the head of a thousand rag-tags, it was easy to imagine him some European general on his way to obscure and bloody battle. But his warriors carried only crude cudgels, battered firearms and blunt swords; they were, nevertheless, in fighting trim.

Cutting through dense woods, his troops suddenly washed up on the edge of a clearing. Confrontation. An opposing band held the high ground, tidily dug in for pitched combat. Quick inventory suggested to the commander that the entrenched bully-boys were better-armed; he knew they were mindlessly nasty and pound for pound,

probably a surer bet in a brawl. Reluctantly, he retired without exchanging a blow.

No, it was not Quebec, Beauharnois or even Queenston Heights. The tiny hamlet of New Glasgow, deep in the forest of Terrebonne County on the rim of Montreal, was simply a polling booth, a convenient spot chosen by Governor General Lord Sydenham to rig the vote for the English Tories in a predominantly French-Canadian riding. Throughout Canada East, Sydenham had slyly stirred the election pot to ensure a tasty English majority in the new legislature.

The year was 1841. This was the first election since the Act of Union of 1840 and placed Canada West (Upper Canada) and Canada East (Lower Canada) under a single assembly. There was no secret ballot, a man stood up to be counted. As a result, candidates frequently brought armed platoons to the polling place – ruffians without the franchise pressed into service because they liked a wrangle. Bribery, intimidation and beatings were an accepted part of the electoral scenario in both Canadas. A man was apt to get his head broken for his political convictions, and at least one unfortunate lost an arm when an enemy zealot hacked it off with his family sword.

The man who looked like Napoleon was Louis Hippolyte LaFontaine – destined to become joint leader of the Province of Canada and eventually a knight of the realm. He had been the member for

THE MAN WOT FIRED THE PARLIAMENT HOUSE!

Punch in Canada singled out Louis LaFontaine (the man who looked like Napoleon) as the one responsible for the riots in Montreal in 1849 and the burning of Parliament. As Leader of the Reform majority, he had authorized the Rebellion Losses Bill that ignited English tempers and sparked arson and violence.

Terrebonne since 1830.

When LaFontaine and his band of supporters were turned back from the polling booth, the English candidate was overwhelmingly elected, leaving the nominal head of the French-Canadian reformers without a seat in parliament. But what at first appeared to be a disaster turned quickly into triumph. In Canada West, Robert Baldwin, leader of the English reform group, found himself elected in two ridings. Knowing LaFontaine's affinity for the union and his earnest desire to work within the system to attain responsible government, Baldwin offered him the safe seat of York South.

powerful triumvirate

From this gesture (a French-Canadian sitting for a Toronto riding!) sprang the root of a powerful triumvirate spanning two provinces and twenty years: Baldwin, LaFontaine and Francis Hincks, Baldwin's lieutenant and close friend.

As politicians, the troika seemed for a time to speak with one voice, but as men they were vitally different. LaFontaine – elegant, artful French-Canadian wrapped in personal success and party charisma; Baldwin – mousey, far-sighted Irish-Canadian plodding down the furrows of his grand dream; Hincks – sparkling, clever Irish-born Canadian conjuring the technical thaumaturgy of high government finance. Separately they might have been merely ambitious powermongers but their combined effort changed Canadian history.

In the uneasy after-birth of union, a faintly sinister breeze blew over a mixed procession of governors-general. First came Charles Poulett Thomson, Lord Sydenham, a fragile suave man ultimately persuasive despite his prosaic mercantile background. Planted firmly in Durham's footsteps to seal the union, Sydenham spun a web of acceptance over the two squawking provinces. Solid Tory that he was, wedded to the Monarchy, he manipulated the 1841 election in ways wondrous to behold and assured himself substantial support in the house.

Kingston, on the shores of Lake Ontario, was chosen as the new capital, a safe compromise between the French strongholds of the east and the still primitive settlements of the west. The governor general met his new assembly in a makeshift but comfortable parliament house rendered from an unused hospital, while he lived at Alwington, a great stone mansion by the water.

After grandly shepherding his major resolutions through the house, confirming at one and the same time the clear responsibility of the governor general to the Crown and of the administration to the people, Sydenham could afford to feel smug. But not for long. On September 4, his horse stumbled just outside the vice-regal residence. Sydenham fell and broke his leg and after two weeks of excruciating pain died of lockjaw.

the Tory conciliator

Next came Charles Bagot whose reputation as a reasonable man preceded him. The *Chronicle* and *Gazette* in Kingston reported the citizens' mood of support for the new governor general – if he would work to one end, "Canada's prosperity," regardless of party.

Although he was Tory to the core, a nephew of the autocratic Duke of Wellington and, at sixty, well past his prime when he arrived, Bagot was determined to encourage co-operation between Reformer and Tory, English and French, all in the interests of the new union. He reached Kingston by sleigh in 1842 in a bitter January frost, and quickly made it his business during the next few months to take the temperature of both Canadas before creating his cabinet for the fall session.

When parliament met, Francis Hincks had accepted the post of inspector-general (roughly com-

YOUNG CANADA
DELIGHTED WITH RESPONSIBLE GOVERNMENT.

James Bruce, the Earl of Elgin (dressed here as a nanny) was the third governor general called to babysit "Young Canada" after the Act of Union opened the way for self-government. He tries to quiet the restive toddler (wearing a toque) with a jumping-jack toy. The playhouse model of the governor's house, Monklands, bears the inscription, "Ici on parlent français." Elgin's predecessor, Charles Metcalfe, frowns his disapproval of such pampering.

parable to minister of finance), and a composite cabinet was formed with William Draper at its head. The wily Draper tried but could not retain the assembly's confidence, and Baldwin and La-Fontaine became co-leaders of a new ministry.

In the midst of his sincere attempts at compromise, Bagot was accused by oldline Tories of "supporting majority rule" (for them an almost mortal sin), an argument so patently ridiculous that he must have despaired. He was damned if he did and damned if he didn't. Under pressure his health broke and he resigned in March, 1843. Six weeks later, before he could return to England, he died at Alwington.

Charles Metcalfe arrived next, driven across the American border in a sleigh pulled by four handsome greys. Deep March snows and icy winds off Lake Ontario shocked him after the steamy heat of Jamaica where he had just recently been governor. Observers described him as "a thorough-going Englishman with a jolly visage." They neglected to mention that his "jolly visage" was ravaged by a cancerous tumour on the left cheek.

Reformers in the saddle

In September 1843, the third session of parliament found the Reform Party firmly in the saddle with sixty seats out of a possible eighty-four. During the sitting the decision was made to move the capital to Montreal, which was expected to become the booming trade centre of a budding new country.

Metcalfe could never truly accept the executive council as the "administration," nor regard them as anything more than advisors. He had ruled in colonial bastions over people of another colour, another time. A clash between Metcalfe's old order and the Canadians' new ambitions was inevitable. The governor general stubbornly forged

This New Year's Day ball invitation mirrored the chaos in politics. Journal Politique *readers in the* bureau *scratch heads, while the throng heeds the banner* "Suivez la foule".

Hatters Hugh Harrison and H. N. Thomson (one a Tory, the other a Radical) advertised the "Union" of their two businesses with fanfare appropriate to the times. Why go across to "Yankee Town" when at the sign of the Cock'd Hat in Belleville you could get any style of topper you wished and support Home Industry at the same time?

ahead making official appointments without consulting the Baldwin-Hincks-LaFontaine trio. They resigned en masse in November and the first salvo in a concentrated campaign to drive Metcalfe from office began.

He was mortally ill but he was a man of great will power and stamina. Trying to run the Canadas with a council headed by William Draper and two prominent French-Canadians, Metcalfe's awkward machine lurched on. No wonder, then, that the election of 1844 was more violent than any held before. It was notable, too, for the first appearance of a young lawyer, John Alexander Macdonald, representing the riding of Kingston.

This time the Tories won by a narrow margin and St. Anne's Market, Montreal, became the House of Parliament. By then, cancer had eaten into Metcalfe's eye. Almost blind, he reluctantly asked to be recalled. The following year, he was dead at age sixty-one, the third governor general in succession to meet a tragic end.

one after another . . .

Inexorably, governor followed governor. Lord Cathcart replaced the dying Metcalfe and then, in 1847, Lord Elgin swept on stage. He was a direct descendant of Robert the Bruce, and son of the British ambassador who salvaged the "Elgin marbles" from the Parthenon and removed them to England, only to be publicly proclaimed a pillager and profligate. Elgin was young as governors come, thirty-six, and poor as aristocrats go: his famous father had impoverished his estates and sired too many children. He was multilingual, a devout Christian, a low-grade conservative by his own admission, yet obviously willing to accept the Canadian obsession with responsible government.

Broad measures were introduced in the parliamentary session of 1849. Baldwin's Municipal Corporations Act still forms the basis of local governments, and Hincks' Guarantee Act inextricably linked Canadian governments with railroads. Legislation for the completion of canals to connect the heartland with the great commercial empire of the St. Lawrence; electoral reform; the creation of non-denominational universities; and an improved judicial system were introduced. But tucked neatly in the agenda was the Act of Indemnification, more commonly known as the Rebellion Losses Bill.

The bill would guarantee compensation for losses suffered by civilians during the rebellions of 1837 and 1838 and offer amnesty to all political offenders.

Here was an explosive charge just waiting to go off. *Were known rebels to be paid in the same coin as staunch loyalists?* English Tories were enraged. The bill was passed by parliament, but they fully expected Lord Elgin to refuse to sign it and pass the problem on to England, where surely past loyalties would count for something.

French-Canadians, radical or temperate, took a very different view. Compensation to them was symbolic of triumph for their nationalism. To discriminate or not to discriminate between rebel and loyalist hardly seemed the question. Meanwhile, the entire issue fermented gently in a rich compost of social unrest.

no pots of gold

In Montreal, warehouses were overflowing with unsold and unmoveable goods, caught in a web of world-wide economic depression. The much touted canal system had failed to deliver the expected pot of gold in either of the Canadas, completed as it was just as the fledgling American railroad network began hauling wares from the West to the eastern *entrepôts*.

Dependent from the outset on British colonial trade policies, Canada was crippled in the forties by the swelling tide of free trade and reluctance on the part of Britons to continue to succour the far-flung empires. The British attitude was characterized by Colonial Secretary Lord Grey writing to Lord Elgin:

To us, except the loss of prestige (no slight one I admit) the loss of Canada would be the loss of little but a source of heavy expense and great anxiety.

But on a broader scale, the economic crisis of 1848 had brought revolutions to Ireland and France. Would the dread political infection spread to the unemployed French and Irish labourers on the Montreal docks? Lord Elgin wrote fretfully to Lord Grey of the "generally uneasy and diseased condition of the public mind."

a certain death knell

The merchants of Montreal were frightened. Sure that their civic authority had evaporated in the ill-wind of reform, and their economic future faced disaster at the very least, they looked on the Rebellion Losses Bill as a certain death knell. While the bill was still before the House, they tried to pressure Lord Elgin to withhold his signature.

Newspaper editors of both provinces were rabid with fear and threats. Ratifying the bill, according to the *Montreal Gazette*, "would raise all Anglo-Saxon blood between Port Sarnia and Gaspé to the 'boiling point'." In Toronto, *The Patriot* thundered:

. . . . we will dare anything rather than submit to the wicked, irreligious principle that the innocent should be taxed to reward the guilty.

When the ice melted on the St. Lawrence and the first ocean vessel surged toward a Montreal dock, the storm broke. Hincks needed the governor general's signature on his new tariff bill to make it effective on cargo about to be discharged.

When Governor General Charles Metcalfe sided with the Tories during the election of 1844, rabid Reformers branded him "Old Square-toes," "the Hindu Despot" and "Charles the Simple."

CANADA *versus* CALIFORNIA.

Hiram. 'Say Zeb! I'm off right slick away for California. My wings is grew, and my nails is mad for diggin!

Zeb. California be bust!—Canada's the washin for me; I guess I'll squat there, where Government pays for Rebellion and no questions axed!

Scores of Canadians fled the depression-bound East with the 'Forty-niners, but Punch's *Zeb is headed north. Rebellion Losses' awards seemed easier pickin's than California gold.*

He sped out to Moncklands, the governor general's residence, on April 25, 1849. Lord Elgin obligingly followed him back to the city to sign several bills, among them, the Rebellion Losses Bill.

A hint of astonishment colours Elgin's report of his departure from the house that day.

When I left the House of Parliament, I was received with mingled cheers and hootings by a crowd by no means numerous, which surrounded the entrance of the building. A small knot of individuals consisting, it has since been ascertained, of persons of a respectable class in society, pelted the carriage with missiles which they must have brought with them for that purpose.

The match was lit, the trail of powder laid and the explosion occurred that night. A citizens' protest meeting in the Champs de Mars turned ugly with cries of "Tyranny!" and "To the Parliament House!" Capriciously, dozens of normally peaceable merchants became an angry mob and rolled westward, pausing only long enough to break windows at the *Pilot*, a reform newspaper.

Reaching the market where the Assembly was in debate, the respectable rabble hurled sticks, stones and brickbats through windows on two sides of the chamber. Members fled in confusion. Not content with chopping up furniture and smashing chandeliers, some misguided wild man set fire to the west wing. Soon the whole building was engulfed in flames and twenty thousand precious books and official papers were lost.

sticks and stones

For the next three days, Montreal trembled under a reign of terror. Members were constantly insulted, knocked down in the street, and LaFontaine himself was so furiously attacked he needed a personal bodyguard just to reach his carriage. Since the parliament house was now gutted, the assembly was moved to Bonsecours Market. The police arrested a number of demonstrators but the widespread destruction continued.

Vandals ransacked LaFontaine's property, cut down his fruit trees, burned his stable and destroyed furniture and books. They were about to fire the new residence when the military arrived and drove them off.

The mercurial crowd met again on April 27 in the Champs de Mars, but their common boiling point dropped a few degrees at the sight of a thousand special constables armed with pistols and cutlasses backed by troops summoned from outlying military posts. Yet the affair refused to die.

souvenir rocks

Lord Elgin, escorted by his suite and a troop of dragoons, rode into town on April 30 to formally receive an address from the assembly stating that his government had conducted itself throughout the uprising with justice and impartiality. He ducked through a harsh rain of stones and rancid eggs to reach Government House – at this point located in the Château de Ramezay – saving a two-pound rock as a souvenir. The mob chased the vice-regal party back to Moncklands, pouring so fierce a barrage of junk that it staved in the carriage and Elgin's brother, Colonel Bruce, received a head wound.

Moncklands was under constant siege while rioters once again looted LaFontaine's property. In the scuffle which followed, a Frenchman killed an Englishman. LaFontaine, ever centre-stage, was tried for complicity in the death but later acquitted.

The infamous April riots cost Montreal her right to be capital of Canada and opened the way for Ottawa, an unpromising outpost still called Bytown.

LITTLE BEN HOLMES AND SOME NAUGHTY CHILDREN ATTEMPT TO PAWN THEIR MOTHER'S POCKET-HANDKERCHIEF, BUT ARE ARRESTED BY POLICEMAN PUNCH, WHO WAS STATIONED "ROUND THE CORNER."

"Naughty" banker Benjamin Holmes and 324 other powerful Montreal businessmen signed the Annexation Manifesto of 1849, calling for Canada's immediate union with the United States.

31

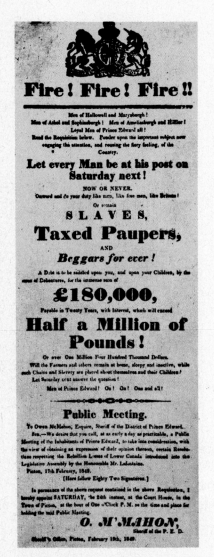

Two months before final passage of the Rebellion Losses Bill, Prince Edward County taxpayers sounded a prophetic note with this broadside ("Fire! Fire! Fire!!") announcing a meeting of public protest.

Comparatively minor demonstrations took place in Quebec City, Toronto, Hamilton and other small towns, but as May blossomed the anger died amid counter-demonstrations, petitions and protestations of loyalty. By refusing to sanction reprisals, Elgin had oiled the turbulent waters and prevented enduring opposition to himself and the constitutional process. The deep emotions stirred by the Rebellion Losses Bill would be long lived, but aside from occasional disturbances, the populace turned to other problems at hand.

charged emotions

Mired in a depression even worse than that of 1836-37, the merchant class of Montreal saw a closer relationship with the United States as the only solution to an economic crisis amplified by the arrival of fifty thousand Irish immigrants stricken with typhus.

Throughout the decade a vague concept of annexation with the United States had persisted. The idea appealed to others besides disillusioned Tories. It attracted *rouge* French-Canadians – the young French radicals with visions of a separate French nation aligned with the United States – along with radical and Tory extremists in Canada West. The summer of 1849 brought emotions to a crescendo after another lean season on the St. Lawrence docks.

The Montreal *Gazette* and three other leading English language newspapers in the city supported annexation while the Annexation Association of Montreal swelled its membership. A small paper in Toronto, the *Canadian Independent* came out for it.

The movement climaxed in October when the Annexation Association issued a startling Manifesto. Listing causes for the "ruin and decay" of Canada's economy, the document called for the "friendly and peaceful" severance from Britain and a union with the United States. The roll of 325 signatures of the manifesto represented the elite of Montreal commerce and included a future father of Confederation, Alexander Tilloch Galt, and a future prime minister, J.J.C. Abbott.

The Montreal manifesto vented the frustration of a vocal minority but prompted a deluge of anti-annexation meetings and declarations. They indicated that the vast majority of Canadians were satisfied with their political institutions, were essentially conservative and carried an ingrained resistence to the United States – with memories of the Rebellions and the War of 1812 still fresh in many minds.

And the political climate was changing. Francis Hincks acted out his final starring role by pushing forward his public works, railway and immigration bills and a repeal of the old navigation laws. Commercial life in Montreal began to perk up and the petulant impulse toward annexation died of malnutrition.

a bid for broader union

By the early fifties, the elder statemen had grown weary of high flight, and a fresh flock of strong-winged frigates poised ready to scoop up the catch. Men like John A. Macdonald, that canny Scot who would hold the reins of power longer than any of his peers; George Brown, stiff-necked reformer carting the doctrine of "rep by pop"; George-Etienne Cartier, revolutionist cum opportunist, who would switch his angle of vision just enough to form a ministry with John A. in 1857. With others, they made a strong bid for a broader union and set the stage of Confederation.

In this building the Canadian Confederation Conference was held It was burned in 1865.

On the night of April 25, 1849, while the House was still in session, an angry mob 1,500 strong stormed into parliament, smashed furniture, tore down drapes and paintings, ripped gas-fixtures from the ceiling and set it ablaze with flaming torches. In 1864, a conference on Confederation was held in the restored building.

33

Cornelius Krieghoff's Quebec

Dutch-born, German-trained, Cornelius Krieghoff arrived in Canada at the age of 25 – a footloose, bohemian artist who had travelled around Europe, served with the U.S. Army in Florida and married a Quebec-born servant girl in New York. After a brief, disappointing sojourn in Toronto in 1840, he set up a studio in Longueuil near Montreal. Small, folksy *genre* paintings were popular gifts and tourist items at the time, and Krieghoff turned them out by the hundreds before his portraits, landscapes and large canvases of rural life and revelry found a market among the well-to-do of Quebec.

Canadiens *working or enjoying* un p'tit coup *of brandy were Krieghoff's most common subjects. This one was sketched at Jean-Baptiste Jolifou's auberge.*

Some critics have scorned Krieghoff's habitant *paintings as "the works of a hack" and "comic mockeries," but at art auctions they still fetch thousands.*

Krieghoff's fine eye for detail is nowhere more apparent than in his 1840 painting, Officer's Trophy Room – a "time capsule" view of the soldier's life in Montreal. Amidst the clutter of pelts, weapons, books, stuffed birds and animals are over two dozen paintings, some possibly by Krieghoff himself.

One of the most extraordinary pieces of fictional art relating to Canada is Stephen Pearce's The Arctic Council Planning a Search for Sir John Franklin *(1851). Pictured at a meeting (which never took place) of the "Council" (which never existed) at British Admiralty headquarters are (left to right): George Back, William Parry, Edward Joseph Bird, James Clarke Ross, Francis Beaufort, John Barrow, Edward Sabine, William Baillie Hamilton, John Richardson and Frederick Beechey. On the wall hang the portraits of Franklin himself, Commander FitzJames and John Barrow, Senior. Four of these men tried unsuccessfully to find the Northwest Passage before John Franklin's ill-fated third voyage, and two tried to locate the missing explorer.*

CHAPTER THREE

Lady Jane's Diary

In Baffin's Land where the whale-fish blows,
Is the fate of Franklin—no one knows.
Ten thousand pounds would I freely give,
To learn that my husband still did live.

Popular ballad, "Lady Franklin's Lament," c. 1850

She encouraged him to go. He was fifty-nine years old, a little weary, a living legend who already had two polar journeys behind him. But she sensed his consuming need to find the elusive strait which would complete the North West Passage and crown his reign as the premier Arctic explorer.

Travel for Lady Jane and John Franklin was the breath of life. Through seventeen years of marriage they were a vigorous, if elitist team, who shared each experience yet frequently separated to fling themselves into opposite corners of the world. When apart, they pitched off countless letters (often panting to catch "the last mail boat") and began every message, "My dearest love."

They complemented each other tidily. John was a fond patriarch with a shy, irritatingly august manner. Lady Franklin was an amicable hostess with a continental flair and a cool eye on the main chance.

Long before noisier, less able women hatched the idea of equality in marriage, Jane Franklin was reaping its benefits. Freedom was natural to both Franklins and so in June, 1845, she watched him sail down the Thames.

The *Erebus* (Franklin commanding) and the *Terror* (Captain F.R.N. Crozier at the helm) had just recently returned from Captain James Ross' venture in the Antarctic. They were stout, square-rigged ships with auxiliary steam engines, and carried a three-year food supply for 134 men. Franklin and the British Admiralty agreed that search parties would be sent out only if no news of the expedition reached England by 1847.

The *Prince of Wales*, a British whaler, met Franklin's ships off the coast of Greenland in late July. Franklin invited the officers to dine the following day, but a sudden breeze cleared the middle ice (great floes coming down Davis Strait between Greenland and Baffin Island) and the ships set sail for the west and Lancaster Sound without the gesture of hospitality.

On this, his third major expedition to the north, Franklin relied on earlier discoveries as well as on his own considerable experience. His thoughtful blueprint for pinning down the passage rested on centuries of incredible lacework patterned by seemingly mad explorers threading their way through ice shrouded channels.

In the sixteenth century, European tastebuds craved pepper and other exotic spices to disguise that appalling staple of their winter diet, salt meat. A handful of citizens with an eye for beauty and fat pocketbooks knew the luxury of silk as well.

While his first wife, Eleanor, lay dying, John Franklin fell in love with her friend, Jane Griffin, and on return from his second Arctic expedition in 1828, the two were married. An independent and strong-willed woman, Jane (above) was an adventurer in her own right, with a record of hair-raising tales from Russia, Greece, Spain and Africa.

John Franklin (1786-1847) – 32 expeditions over ten years probed his mysterious disappearance, eclipsing his fame for two Arctic voyages and his heroics at Trafalgar and New Orleans.

These commodities came from the Far East but the well-travelled road to Cathay was both slow and dangerous. What the world needed in the late fifteen hundreds was a cheap route to China.

Before Franklin there had been Martin Frobisher (a gold-greedy English pirate), Henry Hudson (martyred when his mutinous men cast him adrift), Samuel Hearne (who walked across the top of America) and many others, all assiduously hunting that faster route to the east. They left maps, of course, and rumours – most of them inaccurate.

In 1818, William Edward Parry took the *Hecla* and the *Gripper* deep into polar territory and by observing the Eskimo raised wintering aboard ship to a survival level. In the same year, Franklin struggled overland from Hudson Bay toward the mouth of the Coppermine River. He charted five hundred miles of Arctic coastline – losing eleven men in the process. Back in England, in the fall of 1822, questions were asked and heads were shaken, but John Franklin was well on the way to becoming a holy legend – for he had caught the imagination of the public.

The Admiralty promoted him to captain while the crown gave him a knighthood. Franklin's heart was still in the northland, however. In 1825, he was off again to trace the coastline west of the Coppermine River and if possible, connect Alexander Mackenzie's work in that area with Captain James Cook's explorations from the west through Bering Strait. Accompanied by his friend, Dr. John Richardson, Franklin descended the Mackenzie River to the sea and then struck to the west in two open boats while Richardson turned east. He mapped a thousand miles of shore leaving a gap of only one hundred and sixty miles between his own survey and that of the explorers who had come from the west.

After his return to England, Franklin served in the Mediterranean and was then appointed governor of Van Diemen's Land, a large island off the south coast of Australia, later named Tasmania. With Jane's enthusiastic support, he struggled through the political jungle, but it was obvious that he was better suited to exploring ice. His term ended abruptly under a cloud of disillusionment and charges of incompetence from old rivals in London. When the Admiralty decided to make the final push to solve the riddle of the North West Passage, Franklin lobbied strenuously. He was finally selected to head the expedition despite the fact that he was comfortably past middle age.

True to her nature, Jane Franklin watched her husband set off on his last great adventure, and then taking his daughter, Eleanor, by his first wife Anne Porde, spent the winter of 1845-1846 in Madiera and the West Indies. She was convinced that John was the best navigator in the world and the most experienced Arctic traveller. She had, in 1830, summed up her feelings on the matter in a letter to him:

When all the latent energies of your nature are elicited not I only, but all the world (most proudly I say even literally all the world) knows what you can do and England acknowledged with shouts which almost drowned the declaration, that:

> *In the proud memorials of her fame,*
> *Stands, linked with deathless glory,*
> *Franklin's name.*

In the unforgiving north Franklin's ships first ascended the Wellington Channel, returned along the west side of Cornwallis Island (the entire route being charted) then became ice-bound in a bay near Beechey Island on the north side of Barrow Strait. An ambitious building program – a store-house, workshop, observatory and blacksmith's forge – created an atmosphere of security, but the first faint whispers of disaster were heard. Six hundred tins of preserved meat, the vital staple of their three-year store, were found to be rotten. Back in

At a time when the working man's weekly wage was £1, the British government posted a reward of £20,000 to the rescuers of Franklin and his crew, or £10,000 for news of their whereabouts.

In 1851, John Rae, a veteran explorer for the Hudson's Bay Company, turned up the first clues to Franklin's fate. At Pelly Bay, an Eskimo wearing a gold naval cap-band revealed that a party of thirty gaunt kabloona (white men) had been seen a few years ago headed southward, hauling heavily-laden sledges. The account must have spelled disaster to Rae, a hardy, sensible Scot who had mastered all the survival techniques of the Eskimo and had trekked over 6,700 Arctic miles. His worst suspicions were later verified when another band of natives sold him a silver platter with Franklin's name inscribed, silver forks and spoons, a naval students' manual and other trivia. The bodies found near the booty, he was told, had been badly mutilated, suggesting the party's last desperate attempts to stay alive—cannibalism. With this news Rae returned to London. Eight years later, Francis McClintock (above) found the skeletons.

England, the Admiralty had discovered too late that the brand, *Goldner's Patent*, was a failure and had destroyed large quantities. Three crewmen died that first winter.

The following summer, Franklin worked his ships down Peel Sound in heavy ice, through Victoria Strait and around the west side of King William Island (thought, at the time, to be part of the mainland). There, in September, 1846, the *Erebus* and the *Terror* stuck fast.

unfit for Eskimos

The Franklin ships could not move an inch. Worse, they were trapped in a particularly sterile section of the Arctic – even the Eskimo avoided it. On Monday, May 24, 1847, Commander G. Gore and six men left the ships for King William's Land to hunt for game. Gore deposited a paper in a cairn briefly describing events, and ended: "Sir John Franklin, commanding the expedition, all well."

The well-being was short-lived. On June 11, 1847, Franklin died aboard ship, apparently of natural causes. Two years had elapsed since he set out, and back in England the public mind stirred with uneasiness. Dr. Richard King, a maverick explorer who in 1833 had accompanied Lieutenant George Back along the Great Fish River hunting for the James Ross Expedition, badgered the Admiralty to send out search parties immediately. The Lords of the Admiralty, with the exception of Admiral Beechey, felt no cause for alarm, and Lady Franklin, sure of her husband's transcendent skill, shared their view. She sailed for Italy and spent the month of June sweltering in Rome.

By fall, however, Lady Franklin felt the first twinges of doubt. All her life she had been a prolific letter-writer and she now began a series of extraordinary pleas to the powerful of many countries: Lord Palmerston, Napoleon, the czar of Russia, the president of the United States and a private New York merchant of her acquaintance, Henry Grinnell. (Grinnell later sent out two privately financed expeditions, one in 1850 and another in 1853).

England dispatched a number of vessels in 1848, some approaching from the west through Bering Strait and two, under Captains James Ross and Edward Bird, from the east. Ross ran into heavy ice in Lancaster Sound and proceeded no further.

They were all searching in the wrong area. Both Dr. King and Lady Franklin strongly urged the government to send a land party from the Great Fish River northwest across what is now Adelaide Peninsula to King William Land. A map, enclosed with a letter from Lady Franklin to Viscount Palmerston, shows a square around King William Land, clearly marked "area to be searched".

desperate gambles

As Lady Franklin was pushing for aid from England, the desperate survivors of the *Erebus* and the *Terror* gambled on abandoning the ships. Under Crozier's command, they set out on a trek south in April, 1848, heading for the Great Fish River in the hope of finding game and possibly, itinerant fur traders who might help them to a trading post.

Incredibly, through wind-blown stupidity or strict British naval training, Crozier and his second in command James Fitzjames, burdened their diseased and starving men with an astounding assortment of weighty and unnecessary gear – ten tons of it. They piled their sledges with button polish, silverware, heavy cook stoves, curtain rods, dress swords and even a pair of bedroom slippers – chattels they tossed by the wayside as desperation cut through formality to lighten their load.

John Rae – graduate of Edinburgh, naturalist, marathon explorer and prize-winner for the first Franklin relics. He named Jenny Lind Island.

John Richardson – Franklin's surgeon on the 1825-27 voyage, commander of the first search expedition with Rae until illness forced him to return.

Joseph-René Bellot
Lady Jane's "French Son"

Their friendship must have been the talk of London society in the spring of 1851. *Imagine! Jane Franklin and a French blacksmith's son! And she twice his age! And her husband lost. They say he was wounded in Madagascar, Legion of Honour, too. Charming.* And charmed she was. Judging by Bellot's journal, he was a young gallant: he offered his services "as a son who is in search of his father." Since she had none of her own she accepted, but her letters to him, perfumed with affection, might suggest something more. What became of Joseph-René Bellot? He left for the Arctic in May with former HBC trader William Kennedy (a Scottish-Canadian métis), found no trace of Franklin and returned to Jane. In 1853, aged 27, he tried again, but en route to rendezvous at Lancaster Sound with Edward Belcher drowned.

An inept martinet named Edward Belcher botched up the last naval search mission (1852-54) by getting four of his five ships (including the Assistance *and* Pioneer, *above) stuck in the ice, and was later court-martialled for abandoning them.*

They pressed down the west side of King William Island and found the cairn with Gore's record of the previous year. Crozier added the deaths of Franklin and Gore, as well as news of his own pilgrimage.

At one point, as they straggled wearily over the ice, they met a small party of Eskimo and purchased some seal meat to fit out their dwindling stores. They crossed the narrow strait which separates King William Island from the mainland. South of Cape Hershel the party was forced to leave two dying comrades sheltered in a boat with as much tea and chocolate as they could spare. Their skeletons, and forty pounds of chocolate, were found eleven years later.

At the mouth of the Great Fish River they pitched tents on the small island of Montreal. Too weak to hunt effectively, they resorted to hacking pieces off the dead and attempted to cook them in boots over an open fire. By the time the geese flew north near the end of May, the last few crewmen were scarcely able to bring down half a dozen birds. Debris of feathers and bones was left in mute testimony of their final agony.

In England, Lady Franklin, the Lords of the Admiralty and the legion of Franklin supporters following accounts in the newspapers still hoped survivors would be found. In 1850, the British government sent out Commander Robert McClure in HMS *Investigator* and Captain Richard Collinson in HMS *Enterprise* to sail around the horn, up the west coast of America and approach the polar seas by way of Bering Strait. McClure, an ambitious and rather callous sailor, saw his own star gleaming in the west and followed it determinedly.

Early in the voyage he conveniently lost his companion ship *Enterprise* and pushed on alone. He sailed across the top of Bank's Island to the

One of Belcher's abandoned ships, HMS Resolute, *freed herself from the ice, drifted into Baffin Bay and was towed south by a U.S. whaler. Above, Queen Victoria attends the ceremonious, if humiliating, return of the refitted ship to England.*

Francis Leopold McClintock
The Irish Sledgeman

edge of Melville Sound where he was forced to abandon ship and walk to Beechey Island over the ice. There Edward Belcher's expedition rescued him, and he returned safely to England after spending four winters in the Arctic. McClure was given the accolade of being the first man to complete the North West Passage.

It was Captain Erasmus Ommaney in the *Resolute* who brought the first concrete news of Franklin's party. In 1850, he found the winter camp on Beechey Island. Lady Franklin, spurred to more intensive efforts, convinced that her beloved husband was alive and well and discovering the missing link in the passage, sent out the *Prince Albert* under Captain C.C. Forsyth – but to no avail.

While McClure basked, temporarily, in his aura of achievement, Lady Jane's sure instinct told her the prize belonged to her husband. This cer-

tainty drove her on for seven more years, expending energy and a personal fortune to carve Franklin's special niche in history.

The year 1854 brought the sad news that apparently the entire Franklin party had perished in the snow. Dr. John Rae, sent overland by the Hudson's Bay Company, travelling with sledges toward the mouth of the Great Fish River, fell in with a band of Eskimo. They described a march of emaciated Englishmen, bodies found lying on the ice, some graves and finally, five bodies located on an island at the mouth of the river. Though it was a second-hand report, it had the ring of truth.

The following year, a chief factor of the HBC was sent to the rivermouth and on Montreal Island found relics of the disaster – a silver plate bearing Franklin's initials, a silver spoon with crest and Captain Crozier's initials, and numerous articles from the ship. Even Lady Franklin then real-

The hero in Lady Jane's last effort to close the book on her husband's death was Francis "Paddy" McClintock. Commanding the steam-yacht *Fox*, the short, wiry Irishman and his 25-man crew – 17 of them seasoned Arctic survivors – headed for King William Island. The first eight months were a total loss, the floe-bound *Fox* forced back 1,300 miles by moving ice. By February 1859, the party was back in the search zone, with McClintock (a sledgeman who in 1853 covered 1,408 miles in 105 days) in charge. He designed a light dog-sled, invented a portable stove, cached supply depots en route with pemmican ... in short, he did everything right that Franklin's "naval gentlemen" had done wrong, as they found out when they reached the "graveyard" at Victory Point. Praised, promoted and rewarded for his discovery, he was a pall bearer at Lady Jane's funeral before he died at age 88.

Theatricals, masked balls, boozing and gambling aboard naval vessels broke the monotony of many long, ice-bound winters for officers.

ized there was little hope of finding any of the crew alive. England officially gave up the search (preoccupied with the difficult Crimean situation) but Jane Franklin did not. She sent out the final search party in 1857 under Captain Francis Leopold McClintock, in the steam yacht *Fox*.

noble hopes

She had accepted her husband's death but not his failure. In her letter of instruction to McClintock, she outlined her hopes:

As to the objects of the expedition and their relative importance, I am sure you know that the rescue of any possible survivor of the 'Erebus' and 'Terror' would be to me, as it would to you, the noblest result of our efforts.

To this object I wish every other to be subordinate; and next to it in importance is the recovery of the unspeakably precious documents of the expedition, public and private and the personal relics of my dear husband and his companions.

And lastly, I trust it may be in your power to confirm, directly or indirectly, the claims of my husband's expedition to the earliest discovery of the passage, which, if Dr. Rae's report be true (and the Government of our country has accepted and rewarded it as such) these martyrs in a noble cause achieved at their last extremity, after five long years of labour and suffering, if not at an earlier period.

McClintock was a seasoned Arctic traveller having served with Ross, Belcher and Ommaney and had been made a captain in 1854.

He sailed in July, 1857, and spent the first winter trapped in ice in Baffin Bay. He broke free the following summer and reached Boothia Peninsula where, with an officer named Hobson, he sledged to King William Island. Dispatching Hobson down the west coast, he explored the east side and eventually reached the mouth of the Great Fish River. There he came upon the boat sheltering the skeletons of the two men from Crozier's doomed walk.

At the same time, Hobson located the cairn on Victory Point which held the single document describing Franklin's trials. It was devastatingly casual, yet dramatic in its simplicity. It tersely described Franklin's circumnavigation of Cornwallis Island, the first winter on Beechey Island, Franklin's death and the unrelenting ice which held the ships fast. The document confirmed that Franklin had actually discovered a North West Passage before McClure.

acknowledged in death

Lady Franklin was on the continent when McClintock arrived back in England with his harvest of relics and the unique document. When she returned, she presented McClintock with a silver model of the *Fox* and in her heart at last accepted John's death. For her the struggle ended once officialdom acknowledged that her husband had been the true discoverer of the North West Passage.

A statue of Franklin was erected in his native town, Spilsby, Lincolnshire. The placque described him as the discoverer of the Passage and the seal is placed upon Franklin and his crew's achievement with the words, "They forged the last link with their lives."

Elisha Kent Kane's two insane Arctic expeditions in the 1850s, though reputedly in search of Franklin, had more to do with the business interests of his financier, American shipping and whale oil magnate, Henry Grinnell, and the era's obsession with the North Pole. Kane (above) a hapless, 30-year-old Philadelphia doctor, would have perished if Eskimos and Danish whalers hadn't rescued him. As a youth, he was engaged to Margaret Fox, a clairvoyant.

Paul Kane's Frontier

The new frontier beyond the Great Lakes was a lure to many, including Paul Kane, a Toronto sign-painter and portraitist. Inspired by the works of American artist George Catlin, in June 1845, he set out alone to sketch what he believed were the last remnants of a vanishing Indian culture. His first trip took him as far as Sault Ste. Marie, and a second to the Pacific, yielding 700 sketches. A hundred of these he turned into large canvases before blindness ended his career.

Frederick Verner, who painted this portrait of Kane, was a young artist when Kane's 1848 exhibition (the first glimpse easterners had of the Northwest) opened in Toronto. Verner later made a western sketch tour himself.

On his second journey west, Kane was given carte blanche *by the* HBC's *"Little Emperor," George Simpson, and was treated royally at all posts. At Fort Edmonton, he sketched Cun-Ne-Wa-Bum, this Cree-Métis woman.*

Despite his sincerity and best intentions, Paul Kane had to justify his motives with his Indian subjects, and it wasn't easy. One Ojibwa chief agreed to sit for his portrait only after Kane alleged it would be shown to Queen Victoria (a familiar name). Others, like Caw-Kee-Kee-Keesh-e-ko (the woman with her child, above) thought this clever shaman with colours and brushes would rob them of their most private parts, their souls.

Who's at the door? Cornelius Kreighoff, a painter with a photographer's eye and the wit of Stephen Leacock. While kibitzers and other players try to second guess the man holding the ace of spades, grand-maman shuffles in with tea, a quick-handed tyke swipes an apple and uncle saws an imaginary fiddle.

CHAPTER FOUR

Painters in a New Land

Measures are needed to promote the arts in this province. Our normal schools and secondary schools have no competent drawing masters. . . . It is not surprising then to find our young men go to drink and our young girls to flirt.

Cornelius Krieghoff to A. T. Galt, March 1859

Photography was but a year old in 1840, when a new wave of artists and travellers criss-crossed the country to see for themselves what British North America was really like. The daguerreotype camera, after all, was still a quirky, cumbersome gadget, and no fuzzy tintype miniature was capable of showing the world the wild grandeur of the Northwest and the colour of the eastern provinces.

Fortunately, a few talented artists surfaced in both civilian and military society. Paul Kane produced portraits of western Indians, and William Henry Bartlett rendered careful reproductions of eastern towns and landscapes. William Nichol Cresswell, an English immigrant gentleman farmer, sketched the area around Lake Huron during the 1850s; William Henry Edward Napier's watercolours illuminated the text of the 1857 Canadian government exploring expedition under Henry Youle Hinde and Simon Dawson.

Cornelious Krieghoff captured *habitant* life with a series of lively paintings reflecting the joy of sleighing parties, dancing, drinking and revelry in Quebec inns. His instinct for the peak of the evening when everybody was more than jolly made "merrymaking" his most popular work. He also painted other aspects of local life: the visit from the *curé,* horse-trading in the marketplace and *habitants* racing through tollgates.

Military men like Henry Warre sketched West Coast forts, and Edmund Henderson managed to combine the spare discipline of military draftsmanship with a superbly naive technique. Richard Levinge of the 43rd Monmouthshire Light Infantry and his fellow officer, J.B. Estcourt, recorded regimental sleighing parties in New Brunswick and Lower Canada. G.R. Dartnell, surgeon-general for the British army in Canada, offered views of remote posts like Penetanguishene on the shores of Georgian Bay. Colonel A.C. Mercer carried his sketch-books through Nova Scotia, New Brunswick and Prince Edward Island to bring back rural scenes.

The painters' market in England and Europe often made specific demands upon an artist. William Bartlett was commissioned by a London publisher to produce one hundred and seventeen sketches (later to be made into steel engravings) of the Maritimes and the two Canadas for a book, *Canadian Scenery.*

Somehow, British North America's wild spaces and fragmented settlements had to be shown to

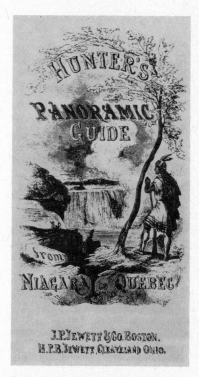

Panoramas were in great vogue at mid-century when American travel artist William Hunter published this guide containing a 12-foot fold-out engraving. James Duncan and Cornelius Krieghoff planned a giant panorama of Montreal as a tourist attraction at about the same time but scrapped the idea.

49

Théophile Hamel
The *Who's Who* Portraitist

At a time when other artists were searching for subjects uniquely Canadian, Théophile Hamel sat in his Quebec studio waiting for his subjects to come to him. And come they did – over 2,000 of them before his death in 1870 at age 53. Born in the Sainte-Foy suburb of Québec, the son of a prosperous farmer, he began taking lessons from Antoine Plamondon (see pages 110-111) at age 17, made the expected hegira to Europe's art capitals, and hung out his shingle in 1846. He priced his portraits high – $100 to $200 a sitting – but well within the reach of his clients, the list of whom reads like a *Who's Who* of Canadian society in the mid-1800s. He worked quickly and precisely, at the best of times completing a portrait a day, a record probably unrivalled by any other artist at the time.

Old World sensibilities. Under Bartlett's cunning pencil, the pioneers' numbing solitude, age producing labour and sparse diet were reduced to serenity, a snug hut and a smoking cook fire. Rough Ottawa Valley loggers became rapids-running heroes – dashing, death-defying and self-sufficient. As their huge log rafts cut through swirling waters, the tent shelter where they cooked, ate and slept remained undisturbed. In the bush, crude frontier homesteads, buried in winter's snow or mired in spring's mud, assumed the dignity of country estates.

Bartlett's advertising was in a worthy cause, however, for the land *was* truly rich and comfortable life was possible. His drawings no doubt soothed many an emigrant's heart before he set out for his final destination somewhere deep in the Canadas.

Bartlett's first New World sketches had been in the United States. He spent the year 1836 touring the eastern seaboard, sketching illustrations to complement a book written by fashionable American journalist, Nathaniel Parker Willis. Within two years, he had the London commission and set out for the Canadas.

agitation ignored

While Lord Durham was travelling through the colonies in the summer of 1838, diagnosing political ills, Bartlett closed his eyes to Canadian recalcitrance, slap-dash architecture, broken roads and poverty-stricken Indians. No trace of agitation marred his careful drawings.

Nevertheless, Bartlett's work was unique. He gave his contemporaries on both sides of the ocean a taste of the new land: the spruce waterfront of Brockville, Canada West; Toronto's busy docks; Quebec City perched on the hill, its harbour bustling with boats and commerce; farms near Kentville, Nova Scotia, which might have been lifted from England's pastoral countryside; Montreal's imposing Notre-Dame Church before the twin spires appeared, and placid lakes and mountains in the Eastern Townships where no wind dared blow. His sketches offered glimpses of a colonial life, scrubbed clean of all unpleasantness.

realist with a mission

Canada's sprawling Northwest was treated by a more realistic artist. Paul Kane, an Anglo-Irish emigrant (he arrived with his parents at the age of nine), considered himself very much a Canadian and a young man with a mission.

As a child, Kane had grown up in "Little York." After a rather shaky start painting furniture in Cobourg, Upper Canada, and portraits in New Orleans, Kane scratched together sufficient funds for an artist's tour through Italy's art galleries. He sailed for Europe in 1841. Two years and dozens of galleries later, he ended up in London, England where chance drew him to George Catlin's exhibition of American Indian paintings.

Catlin's work touched a spring in Kane which set his mind in motion. By early 1845, Kane was back in Canada, determined to go west.

The North American Indian was no new subject for painters, but prior to Kane most works showed the western tribes as faceless curiosities, people whose customs and culture exemplified their primitive way of life. But the white man's view of the native was changing, and Kane was in the forefront – more interested in the people than in documenting their traditions.

He set out alone with only his paints, guns and ammunition to sketch some Ojibwa chiefs in Great Lakes country. The difficulties and risks of travel convinced him he would need assistance. At Sault Ste. Marie, he so impressed the local Hudson's Bay Company factor, John Ballenden, that the trader recommended him to George Simpson, then

Painting paintings within paintings has long been a common (and sometimes comic) twist employed by artists. In his painting, The Studio (1845), *could it be that Cornelius Krieghoff is twisting the viewer's imagination even further by painting a picture of himself painting a picture of himself . . .?*

51

Although most art historians either ignore the works of William Henry Bartlett, or dismiss them as the hackneyed impressions of a romantic traveller, as a visual record of the 19th century Canada they have considerable value. If many of his views are similar to this one of Cobourg, it is because most towns were.

chief overseas officer of the company. In May 1846, Simpson authorized Kane's travels to the West Coast with the fur brigades. Simpson urged Kane specifically to paint the Métis on their annual buffalo hunt south of the Red River settlement and commissioned about a dozen paintings.

Travelling in the relative safety of HBC canoes, Kane began recording Indian life in earnest, and his diary, *Wanderings of an Artist*, revealed not only his profound regard for Indian courage and pride but the uglier side of tribal life as well.

patience and trinkets

Important chiefs often refused to pose, believing a "likeness" would rob them of part of their souls. Kane overcame such resistance with patience, trinkets or by the ruse of ignoring his subject who then might beg petulantly to be sketched.

Travelling along the shore of Lake of the Woods, Kane was astounded to see one hundred and fifty miles of forest stripped bare by an army of green caterpillars. Smaller insects made an equally strong impression: "I found it indispensibly necessary to wear a veil all day," he wrote as he visited an Indian encampment along the Brokenhead River, "as protection from the mosquitoes which I had never before seen so numerous."

He enjoyed a meal of fish at the camp – cooked in water-filled birch bark bowls into which hot stones had been dropped – and examined the tribe's unique hieroglyphics enscribed on strips of the bark.

Upon reaching Fort Garry, Kane was eager to join a buffalo hunt and fulfill Simpson's commission. As he rode to catch up with a roving band of Métis hunting south of the American border, Kane crossed the plains "carpeted with wild roses."

Sketch book and pencil at the ready, Kane caught up with two hundred Métis in search of a major herd. Before they broke camp one morning, a dozen local Sioux chiefs paid a visit to smoke a pipe and negotiate peace. (Sioux and Métis had fought a fitful war for years). The discussion was interrupted by the discovery of a freshly scalped Métis. Only the intervention of wiser and cooler heads prevented young comrades of the victim from taking instant revenge. Three days farther along the trail, the angry Métis ambushed a Sioux scouting party, killing eight braves.

"Though differing in very few respects from the pure Indians," Kane reported solemnly, "they (Métis) do not adopt the practice of scalping." Small comfort. They abandoned the dead Sioux to a party of what Kane called "Saulteaux" tribesmen who earlier had joined the main hunt. Kane wrote: "One old woman, who had lost several relations by the Sioux, rendered herself particularly conspicuous by digging out their eyes and otherwise dismembering them."

the great buffalo carpet

These experiences were only a prelude to a remarkable buffalo hunt. Scouts brought word of a herd numerous enough to carpet the prairie to the horizon. The animals were within six hours ride, so Kane and a Métis friend set out for a preview.

Kane was able to sketch a great herd of between four thousand and five thousand bulls grazing sedately, apart from their cows. The Métis walked their horses slowly toward the herd while each brave filled his mouth with shot, which "he drops into the gun without wadding; by this means loading much quicker and being enabled to do so whilst his horse is at full speed." Once the buffalo caught human scent, they thundered off and the hunters spurred their mounts in hot pursuit.

In twenty minutes, Métis and buffalo were mixed in such confusion that hunters shot each

William Henry Bartlett
The Itinerant Draughtsman

England, Europe, Canada, the U.S. and Asia – William Henry Bartlett sketched them all, sent his works to engravers and saw hundreds of thousands of copies spill from the printing presses during his lifetime. Born in England in 1809, at 14 he was articled to architect John Britton as a draughtsman. His work first appeared in *Cathedral Antiquities of England* and a sequel, *Picturesque Antiquities of English Cities,* published by Britton in 1830 and 1832. Between 1836 and 1852, he made four sketching trips to North America, touring the eastern States and Canada from Halifax to Niagara. *Canadian Scenery* was published in 1842 in two volumes, with text by the American travel writer, N. P. Willis, and engravings based on the hundreds of drawings Bartlett had made of towns and sights. He died at sea, en route home from Asia.

A decade before Paul Kane made his trek through the West, a 27-year-old Swiss artist named Karl Bodmer painted this Assiniboine chief's portrait in what is now southern Saskatchewan.

other by accident. Bits of apparel brought especially for the purpose were dropped on carcasses to identify the successful hunter's kill. The chase lasted an hour and ranged over six square miles. In the end, five hundred buffalo lay dead or dying.

Having killed one huge buffalo, victory went to Kane's head. In the midst of the chaos he hit a second "enormous animal" which refused to fall. Kane felt an irresistible urge to preserve the moment for history; he wrote:

The blood was streaming profusely from his mouth, and I thought he would soon drop. The position in which he stood was so fine that I could not resist the desire of making a sketch. I accordingly dismounted and had just commenced when he suddenly made a dash at me.

Kane snatched up his gun and supplies, remounted and chased the bull into the heart of the action. He managed to hit it again and "this time he remained on his legs long enough for me to sketch."

no debauchery

Returning to the relative quiet of the HBC posts, Kane wrote in his diary that he witnessed no debauchery or drunkenness at the company enclaves. He noted that the Métis were inclined to grumble although the company treated them with "great liberality." When times were hard, he reported, HBC officials offered assistance; in sickness they furnished medicine and in times of conflict acted as mediators between hostile bands.

Kane arrived at Fort Carlton on the North Saskatchewan River in early September and found it under siege by the powerful Blackfoot. When horses were put out to pasture, the Blackfoot stole them. To repel the thieves, the Baymen had mounted blunderbusses on each bastion. While they sweated out a vigil, a band of friendly Crees took refuge inside the palisades to swap tales of better days when the Blackfoot had been their slaves.

Kane moved on to Jasper House in the foothills of the Rockies, which he described as "three miserable log huts." Its sole purpose in the great HBC scheme of things was to provide horses for mountain crossings. The main dwelling consisted of two rooms, each fifteen feet square. One room was used by travellers of both sexes and all ages while the other belonged to the company official, Colin Fraser, his Cree wife and their nine children. On his return to the east in the fall, Kane was terrified of being trapped at Jasper House by snow and cold weather.

firewood and furs

Each year the HBC delivered a precious cargo of choice furs to the Russian American Company on the northern coast of what is now British Columbia, in return for trapping privileges in Russian territory. Kane accompanied the HBC men and their shipment as they struggled through mountain passes on snowshoes. The horses were sent back almost immediately because of deep snow. Overnight camps were established by stamping down the waist-high snow with snow-shoes. Six twenty-foot logs were cut to make a platform and a fire was kindled in the center. Men wrapped themselves in blankets, feet towards the fire, and lay upon mattresses of pine branches. The firewood was arranged so that the green logs would not burn through until morning.

Once on the coast, Kane sketched Indian life around Fort Vancouver, Vancouver Island and on the mainland. While he found costumes, dances and hunts colourful and Indian faces forceful and proud, he viewed many local customs with distaste.

Several coastal tribes kept slaves which they

Kane's travels on the Coast during the winter of 1846-47 ranged from Fort Vancouver on the Columbia (Oregon) to the area of Prince Rupert, where he sketched this Babine (Carrier) chief.

Pictorial lids on pots of cosmetics and hair pomades (generally made from bear grease) reflected the public's fascination with the West. At the Great Exhibition (World's Fair) in London in 1851, this pot-lid, based on a painting by George Catlin (Paul Kane's idol) covered the jars of an American exhibitor.

seized from the Chastays, a small tribe that lived south of the Columbia River, or bought them from Chastay parents. The Babines, another small tribe identified by Kane, inserted a slender piece of bone in the lower lip of infants and gradually enlarged it until it was a three-inch disc which caused the lips to "protrude frightfully."

obliging fellows

None of these strange practices went unnoticed. In one tribe, Kane wrote, the woman was strapped to the body of her dead husband, covered with skins and placed with him on a burning pyre. At the point where she almost suffocated, she was released so she could restore falling pieces of the burning corpse to their original position—with her bare hands. Fellow tribesmen obligingly wailed and beat a drum tattoo to smother her shrieks of pain.

When the corpse was reduced to a handful of ashes she collected them, placed them in a bag and wore it on her back for three years. This custom led other Indians to call the tribe "Carriers." During the next three years, the widow was a slave to her husband's relatives and was prevented from washing or combing her hair.

After the mourning period, relatives and friends stripped the woman naked, covered her with fish oil and feathers and compelled her to join a grisly dance around a pole supporting a box containing her husband's ashes. She was then free to remarry and again risk widowhood.

On Kane's return journey east, he saw ten thousand buffalo in a single herd. The beasts were so bogged down in snow that they stood dead still and faced their fate without flinching. The hunters finally tired of such easy sport and retired from the slaughter. One enormous bull took sixteen bullets to fell, and Kane recorded that it died "harder than I had ever seen an animal die before."

He spent Christmas Day, 1847, at Fort Edmonton where the dining hall was one of Tartarian splendour. Large fires warmed the fifty-by-twenty-five-foot room with boarded walls painted in "barbaric gaudiness" and ceiling "filled with centre-pieces of fantastic gilt scrolls." The festive meal featured boiled buffalo hunch, boiled and smoked unborn buffalo calf, dried moose nose, white fish browned in buffalo marrow, beaver tails, roast wild goose, potatoes, turnips and bread. During the evening, guests, company officials, Indians with painted faces, voyageurs in bright sashes and Métis glittering with ornaments danced to a fiddler. Kane was so smitten by Cum-ne-wa-Bum ("one that looks at the stars") that he painted her complete with white feathered fan.

praiseworthy portraits

When Kane's Toronto exhibition opened in November 1848, in the old city hall on Front Street, it offered two hundred and forty pieces, many in oil and watercolours, as well as Indian artifacts—carved masks, Babine blankets, a painted buffalo robe and a Northwest Coast cedar hat purchased at Fort Victoria for a little over one pound.

Reviews were generally good. The *British Colonist* praised some portraits, especially one of a Blackfoot chief on a grey horse, and George Brown's *Globe* stiffly noted it had no doubt that Indian portraits and northwestern scenes were "particularly accurate."

Moon-light and fire-light cast eerie shadows across the painted faces of these celebrants in the ritual scalp dance of the Spokane Indians. Besides the 700-sketch record of his journey, Kane also kept a journal, published in 1859 as Wanderings of an Artist among the Indians of North America.

Two steamers on the Bay of Fundy run, and a fleet of sleek square-riggers, vie for wharf space in the crowded harbour of Saint John, New Brunswick's commercial capital. Shipbuilding, lumbering and fishing industries witnessed record peaks and abysmal lows in the two decades in all Atlantic colonies.

CHAPTER FIVE

A View from the Harbour

The capital of Nova Scotia looks like a town of cards, nearly all the buildings being of wood. There are wooden houses, wooden churches, wooden wharfs, wooden slates, and, if there are side walks they are of wood also.

I. L. Bishop, The Englishwoman in North America, 1856

While Canada East and West were doing their best to live happily ever after under the terms of Union, Britain's four Atlantic colonies seemed destined to struggle alone toward a better way of life. Some said history and geography were to blame.

The port towns of Halifax and Saint John, Charlottetown and St. John's continued to look to the sea, but more often than not when the ships came in, the cargo and passengers were headed for Quebec, Montreal, Kingston or Toronto. The fertile farmlands and booming milltowns of "Upper Canada" (any place west of the New Brunswick border) siphoned off the mainstream of immigrants with promises of an easier life and higher wages.

Alexander Monro, long an inhabitant of Baie Verte near the New Brunswick-Nova Scotia boundary, summed it up in 1855:

One of the principal reasons for so little having been done commensurate with this extent of resources and capability for development is the ignorance of the true character of these Provinces.

He quoted a British schoolboy who asked how far it was from Halifax to Nova Scotia, and complained that at the 1851 London World's Fair, New Brunswick was represented by "a lump of asphaltum, the figure of an Indian and a bark canoe." At the New York Exhibition not long after, "this province was represented solely by two beaver hats and a box of biscuits."

While England might be unfamiliar with many of the resources in New Brunswick, she knew one thing: a pristine colony covered with ships' masts just waiting for the axe was a prize possession. The Baltic states and Norway could not always be counted on in time of war, and therefore England granted New Brunswick timber a protective tariff which spurred the industry.

It was this same precious timber, however, which would eventually spark spats between local government officials, merchants and independent lumbermen during the mid-nineteenth century. Descendants of those early Loyalists felt entitled to a healthy share of prosperity when it swept in with the sale of white pine. Having survived the harsh climate and bruising poverty in the absence of civilizing influences, they felt any money made from the rich timber grants should go to their own kind. That much was clear – and then came Baillie.

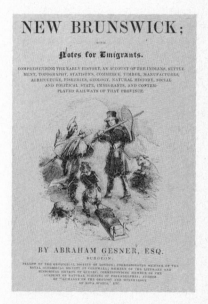

Born in Cornwallis, Nova Scotia, the son of a Loyalist, Abraham Gesner was a man of diverse and remarkable talents (as his fine-print credits, above, attest). Surgeon, historian, geologist and surveyor of Prince Edward Island and New Brunswick, he discovered kerosene in 1853, and patented its first extraction process. His book on New Brunswick appeared in 1847.

The Incredible Signor Blitz

Ladeez and Genulmen . . . the Amazing, the Incredible, the Astounding . . . Signor Blitz! The "carny's" patter was the same well over a century ago when the first travelling magic shows and menageries rolled into town. These were the first (and sometimes the only) popular entertainments in most towns and villages, and young and old alike flocked to the performances. The troupes and itinerant actors were almost all Americans—sleight-of-hand artists of the pre-vaudeville circuit who could pick a sucker's pocket as easily as pull a dozen rabbits from a hat. Animal acts were always a big drawing-card: trained fleas, talking dogs, baby elephants, educated canaries and dancing bears (among other talent). Apparently Signor Blitz, whose act played at the Mechanics' Institute in Saint John, New Brunswick, in June of 1853, was well-known across Canada and the U.S. When Arctic explorer Elisha Kent Kane (see page 45) returned from his first trip to the North in 1851, and went on the road to advertise his feats, he got second billing one evening between Signor Blitz's canaries and the famous American essayist Henry David Thoreau. Poor Dr. Kane. A bird pulling a wagon and firing a cannon is a pretty tough act to follow, to say nothing of the rest of Blitz's Saint John extravaganza and the finale, the "Dance of Six Plates on a Common Table!"

Thomas Baillie was appointed commissioner of crown lands for New Brunswick in 1824, and in the sixteen years he ruled, Baillie was hated by both rich and poor. Only a few important merchants circumvented his unique power to grant or deny them cheap timber berths. The sale of crown land was simply intended to fill imperial coffers back in London but his arrogant attitude to the local aristocracy brought threats of assassination. As small lumbering companies struggled to survive, they grew to despise his witholding of timber berths, exorbitant charges for cutting rights and demands for bribes. Local politicians chopped his $10,000 salary in half as soon as legislation made it possible.

Before his final curtain call in 1851, Baillie had ruined many men but he had strengthened the formidable Cunard brothers, Samuel, Joseph and Henry, with a grant of 500 square miles of prime timberland along the Miramichi. When their arch-rival Alexander Rankin complained about the obvious favouritism, Baillie offered him an equally vast timber reserve along the Restigouche.

final favours

Baillie and Samuel Cunard were also linked in the New Brunswick and Nova Scotia Land Company, formed in March 1831, when both men negotiated with the London Colonial Office for 350,000 acres of New Brunswick land at three shillings an acre. The following year the same company acquired another half-million acres at two shillings, three pence each.

Baillie's friend Samuel Cunard was not entirely dependent on crown grants to build his enormous empire, though the timber rights helped considerably. Sam was cut out for business from the time he was a mere lad. His father Abraham, a staunch Loyalist, founded the A. Cunard Company with a single schooner built in Charlottetown, P.E.I. Besides the company, Samuel inherited from his father the ability to be tough, far-sighted and manipulative, and the willingness to take risks.

For all the Cunard brothers, business was an ever-expanding affair. Samuel put steam ships on the Pictou-Charlottetown run as early as 1832, when many shipping lines considered steam a joke. When news spread in 1833 that the *Royal William* had crossed the Atlantic under steam power alone, Samuel Cunard saw the future of ocean travel revealed. When the age of steam hissed in, Cunard was ready. By 1841, Cunard Shipping Lines had four steamships in service on the Atlantic, and when the new schedule was announced in 1848, two Cunard steamers crossed the ocean each week:

While New Brunswick was riddled with internal bickering, she also suffered pressure from outside. There was the ongoing dispute about the Maine-New Brunswick boundary. Valuable timberland along the St. Croix River in the Madawska area was the cause of a minor, somewhat farcical fray called the Aroostock War. In 1838, when Canadian and American loggers took to beating each other up over this precious territory, the incidents threatened to escalate into an international scrimmage. In 1842, Daniel Webster and Lord Ashburton representing America and England, signed the Webster-Ashburton Treaty and established the present border between Maine and New Brunswick.

erratic schedules

In the 1840's, people travelling from the Maritimes to Canada voiced many of the same complaints heard nearly a century before when the country lived under the governors of New France. Granted, steam-driven paddle-wheelers now made the voyage up the St. Lawrence (except in winter, of course), but schedules were at best erratic. The alternative route, by stage coach through New Brunswick, may have been passable in dry weather for lumber wagons and mail carts, but those who survived the trip cursed the road for being "in such a state as to frighten both man and beast."

never on Sunday

Sending a message from Halifax to Saint John or Fredericton (or, God forbid, having to make the trip yourself) was no less an ordeal. By stage the journey took at least forty-six hours. If the steamer from Windsor was running, the direct route – across the Minas Basin and the Bay of Fundy – only took twenty hours. But never on Sunday.

It was not surprising, then, that when Canadian and Atlantic delegates met at the first Intercolonial Conference in Halifax in 1849, few of them could agree on anything. Leaders of the old colonial "family compacts" were on the run, hounded by young upstart liberals and reformers, the likes of Joe Howe of Nova Scotia, Edward Whelan of P.E.I., Lemuel Allan Wilmot of New Brunswick, and John Kent of Newfoundland.

All the colonies, each in their separate way, were trying to make some sense out of this new and baffling notion of "responsible government." New Brunswick and P.E.I., beset by hard times, were talking about trading off inshore fishing rights to the United States for access to eastern American markets. And fanatics went as far as calling for annexation to the U.S.

For all the wrangling, the conference wasn't a total waste of time. Those delegates with a bit of foresight saw the beginning of the railway boom in Canada as a means toward Maritime prosperity. Telegraph lines from Toronto had reached Quebec two years ago and now stretched as far as Rivière du Loup. The hook-up with Saint John and Halifax would be a simple matter – and after that, perhaps, an intercolonial railway.

**Edward Whelan
Orphan of the Palladium**

There must have been something about the 14-year-old Irish lad, standing by his mother on the Halifax wharf, that attracted Joe Howe, for within days of their meeting, young Edward Whelan was working as an apprentice at the *Novascotian,* reading still-wet editorials by his boss, and learning about colonial printing and politics. In 1842, P.E.I. Reformers, fed-up with corrupt government and eager to throw off the shackles of absentee landlords, were looking for a writer to publicize their cause, and Howe sent them 19-year-old Whelan. Though his first paper, the *Palladium,* died in 1845, Whelan won election to the P.E.I. assembly the following year and was back in print in the *Examiner* a year later. His personal life was filled with tragedy (all his children died young), but before his untimely death at 43, he saw self-rule on the Island and Canada's Confederation.

British regiments remained in the colonies throughout the '40s and '50s, but wars overseas kept their ranks low. Above, officers stationed in New Brunswick, with nothing better to do, are headed for a night of revelry at the Blizzard Inn.

The Canadian winter continued to confound tender-footed immigrants (especially the well-to-do) from warmer British climes. This sketch of an army officer's winter dress, contributed by an almost-anonymous Mr. S. to an English journal, was accompanied by the following note: "The winters here are very severe. Everything that comes to market is stiff. In one night water freezes many inches...and often the streets are so slippery that it is impossible in any ordinary way to walk. Creepers (an iron bar with two teeth, strapped to the shoe) are then used."

It should have been a simple matter, but it wasn't. When Frederick Gisborne, a brilliant twenty-six-year-old engineer and superintendent for the British North American Electric Telegraph Association, offered to extend the company's lines across New Brunswick, the Fredericton legislature looked on the offer as a "Canadian plot." Why should the province foot the bill when an American company was willing to connect Saint John with their line from Boston via Portland, Maine, *gratis*?

While New Brunswick's money men backed the U.S. connection, Nova Scotians seemed to be of a different mind. Coaxed by Joe Howe into confidence that the B.N.A. line from Toronto would someday go through, the Halifax-Amherst connection was approved and completed in November 1849.

The wire was not left dangling at the New Brunswick border. From Sackville the line ran south to Calais and into Maine, and the first message pecked out by the telegrapher in Halifax was a European dispatch for Associated Press of New York. Gone were the days of the pony express from Halifax to the Digby-Saint John ferry. As fast as Samuel Cunard's steamers could bring the news to the Nova Scotia docks, it was on the wire to the American capitals. It would take thirty years before Montreal and Toronto got their messages direct from Halifax.

By 1856, all the petty sectionalism and red tape over the telegraph issue was forgotten, and Peter Hamilton, editor of the *Acadian Recorder*, proclaimed a new spirit of cooperation among the Maritime colonies:

The natural barriers which once separated these Provinces from each other, are now in a great mea-

Downtown Halifax around 1840: the Dartmouth ferry has just pulled into its slip and the market is busy with farmers and fishermen selling their produce to townsfolk and one Micmac woman (centre foreground) in her pointed cloth hat.

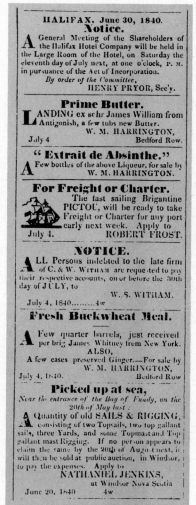

A glimpse of everyday life in the port of Halifax during the first week of July 1840 – nothing earth-shattering, just business. The same issue of the Acadian Recorder *carried the inauguration notice for Samuel Cunard's British and North American mail-steamer line.*

sure removed. The communication between any two of the Provinces is now almost as free as that which exists between the different parts of any one of them; and an immediate effect of their political Union would be to make it quite as much so . . . .

Almost forgotten, too, was all the haggling over what everyone considered the real vehicle for unity, the intercolonial railway. Parts of it were finally under construction.

When the railway issue first came up in 1846, both Nova Scotia and New Brunswick were optimistic that London would pick up the construction tab. Two years later, when the survey from Halifax to Quebec was completed and Britain paid the bill, it seemed success was just around the bend.

High spirits were dampened somewhat in 1850, when Colonial Secretary Earle Grey announced that the money from London would not be forth-coming, but coincidentally an American railway promoter named John Alfred Poor had an alternate scheme. If England didn't care about her colonies' well-being, *he* would see to it that Maritime railways were linked up with the north-south flow of commerce through the "future capital of the Atlantic," Portland.

The Poor plan was unveiled in all its glory on July 31 in Portland with pageantry and banquets fit for kings. Now all that Maritimers would have to do would be to come up with the money and build their rail line to the American border.

Joe Howe shuffled off to London and somehow convinced the Colonial Office to at least lend the colonies the revenue to start the project. A month later, in December, however, when the colonial secretary realized that the line was really an American proposal, the promise of credit was scotched. The colonies would have to go it alone.

Major John Thomas Lane's
INDIAN REMEDIE.

A CERTAIN CURE and PREVENTION of SMALL POX. Never fails, and leaves no Scars on the Face, as thousands of Certificates will testify. Perfectly harmless, as Children of all ages have taken it.

MOO-ZOO-MONY, Or Rice Gatherer, CHIEF OF THE CHIPPEWAS.

JOHN THOMAS LANE, Medicine Man, Chief and Colonel of the Mic-Macs, Discoverer and Proprietor of the Indian Remedy for the Cure and Prevention of Small Pox.

ALSO:
Proprietor of J. T. LANE'S Celebrated INDIAN LINIMENT or PANACEA for Rheumatism, Neuralgia, Putrid Sore Throat, &c.; and his celebrated MIC-MAC PILLS, for Dyspepsia and all Stomach Diseases, now in general use, and patronized by principal persons of Europe and America.

They did their best. The economic slump of the late forties released its grip, and by 1853, prices for New Brunswick lumber had doubled. Maritime drydocks enjoyed peak production, and P.E.I. products found ready buyers throughout the region. Newfoundland, which had been largely unaffected by hard times, continued to bank the profits from record catches, paying cash on the barrel for what the other provinces had to sell.

Poor progress

And the railway? It was slowly being built in bits and pieces, but without the help of Mr. Poor. True to his name, he had no money. The lines from Halifax to Truro and Windsor were finished in 1857 and 1858. By 1860, the track from Saint John reached Shediac, and the sleepy town of Moncton was already claiming itself more than just a whistle stop. The rest of the Intercolonial, the main line linking the Maritimes to Quebec, would not be built until after Confederation, but an important start had been made.

At a banquet in Montreal after the turn of the decade, Edward Whelan, the young firebrand editor of the Charlottetown *Examiner*, summed up the two decades with his usual candour:

In the Colonies we have been strangers to each other too long . . . We have been jealous and apprehensive of each other; mutually restricting our trade and placing obstacles in the way of our prosperity, not knowing and not respecting each other as we should.

All that, he hoped, was past history.

Although smallpox vaccine had been available in Canada since 1801, some of our gullible ancestors still fell prey to quack medicine ads like this one from Halifax's British Colonist *around 1860. The ad forgets that all Indian "remedies" failed to combat the smallpox epidemics that ravaged eastern tribes in the late-1600s and 1700s.*

Tin fireplace reflectors, buttons, knives, cheap jewelry, polyglot bibles and a hundred other notions were unveiled by pedlars on their rounds. In the Maritimes, the Yankee clock salesman (immortalized in Haliburton's classic, The Clockmaker) *was the most notorious of this silver-tongued breed.*

Bytown to Milltown

Throughout the 1840s, canals and mills continued to play an essential part in Canada's development from a pioneer to an industrial society. The ambitious canal-building programme of the two previous decades, which saw the Rideau, Welland and Lachine canals built, was revived, and the St. Lawrence

With a military engineer's precision, Henry Francis Ainslie drew this view of the massive stone locks of the Rideau Canal at Bytown (Ottawa). Colonel By's costly engineering masterpiece became somewhat of a "white elephant" when the more direct St. Lawrence canal system siphoned off most commerce.

waterway to Windsor was completed by 1850 to a navigable depth. Along rivers flowing into the system, mills seemed to spring up at every falls and rapids. In Canada East and West over a thousand grist mills were grinding away in 1852, to say nothing of the 2,000 saw mills, 100 woollen mills and a dozen paper mills scattered throughout the Province. In the good times of the mid-forties, wheat exports from the western (Ontario) breadbasket nearly tripled to 3.3 million bushels, most of it shipped down the St. Lawrence to Britain. The challenge from steam engines and railways was yet to come.

The McDonell brothers' Ganonoque Mills near Kingston were typical of grist mills of the period. Though artist Ainslie's curious perspective doesn't show the interior, Richard Bonnycastle, an 1841 visitor, pronounced the machinery "most expensive and complicated" and the flour "deservedly celebrated."

Upper Canada's oldest "railway" – the Erie and Ontario – started service with horse-drawn carriages in 1839. In 1854, the line bought its first steam engine for the short run from Niagara-on-the-Lake to Chippewa, and in the 1860s, when this scene at the Falls was painted, was part of the Canada Southern.

CHAPTER SIX

The Coming of the Iron Horse

After the last toast had been drunk . . . the company left to resume their seats in the cars. They found, however, that most of the space had been occupied by a motley crew of persons belonging to places along the line who willy-nilly were determined to make their way in comfort to their destinations. . . .

Inauguration of Toronto-Oshawa service of
Grand Trunk Railway, Toronto *Globe*, August 25, 1856

Not a single strip of iron rail fractured the three thousand mile expanse between Halifax and Fort Langley on the Fraser River's shore. Through the stern territories of British North America. . . . the lonely Maritime shores, sullen Laurentians, lush waterways of the St. Lawrence and Great Lakes, paper-flat prairies and redoubtable Rockies . . . no all-season artery bound isolated communities together.

Canadians knew track couldn't be laid in wilderness, swamp and mountain pass. While railroads spread like vines in England and the United States, the idea was unthinkable in this harsh northland under British control.

Then one hot July night in 1837, the *Kitten*, a balky little steam engine built in England and assembled in Montreal, made her somewhat truculent debut. Nervous benefactors tested her under the secrecy of moonlight. True, she refused at first to budge and had to be cozened with more wood

and water. But she *went*. That was the important point. She eventually rattled along the wooden rails between Laprairie on the south shore of the St. Lawrence and St.-Jean on the Richelieu River, at an amazing twenty miles an hour.

The *Kitten* was top-heavy, her stack a long-stemmed mushroom, her centre of gravity too high, and her coaches open to the breeze. And she was skittish. Even after her glorious initial run, horses often had to be dragooned to pull coaches and freight. But once a schedule was established it became the thing to do to day-trip out of Montreal and picnic on the rail lines (this whimsy was firmly disciplined), climb on the engine, (a ten shilling fine) and even drag pets along (no canines in first class, please).

Samson arrived in 1839 – capable of pulling thirty-two cars up a steep hill, with a load of three tons each and pulling over four hundred tons on a level track. Built in Shildon, England, *Samson* was the first locomotive in British North America to burn coal and run on an all-iron track. The 38,000 pound pride of the General Mining Association of Stellarton, Nova Scotia, *Samson* hauled coal from the Albion Mines along the six miles of rail to the loading docks at Dunbar Point.

When the short run was in full operation, a wooden passenger car was added to conduct mining officials to and from the mines. One of the first passengers on the elaborate coach was the bride of

Newspapers of the period brimmed with stock offers for shares in real and "paper" companies. Crammed in every available inch of space with the promoters' ads, foundries sold rails, spikes, engines and other hardware to the budding companies.

the governor-general. The car soon became known as the "Bride's Coach," and it was said that if young lady passengers could ride in the coach without uttering a word for twenty minutes, they would find a husband within the year.

To men of vision, railroads were more than just convenient portages. Gazing into their crystal balls they saw *money* and the sight blinded them to obvious difficulties. For the most part they were politicians, lobbyists, contractors and risk-takers, but in the dim light of the times, they were also seers.

eccentric arrogance

Who *were* these men who rushed ahead, juggling contracts and land grants, creating scandals even as they created railroads in the unyielding countryside? Each entrepreneur who helped spawn Canada's rambunctious railway system was in some way extraordinary. Often arrogant, grasping and eccentric, they were constantly accused of self-seeking (as members of parliament the directors of newly chartered railroads voted themselves more charters and government financial support). Yet, however grating, they were necessary for the task.

These ramrodders of the early railways seemed perfectly fashioned for the part . . . an exotic blend of pretentious power-wielders and grandiloquent dreamers with an acquired taste for the taxpayers' money. Alexander Tilloch Galt, Francis Hincks, George-Etienne Cartier, John A. Macdonald and Allan Napier MacNab were all elected representatives who just happened to become directors of railroad companies. What if MacNab, as one of the staunchest Tories in Parliament, offered MacNab, as president of the Great Western Railway, desperately needed financial support? If the government was a money-tree, well, the harvest of the railways would justify it.

While Allan MacNab suitably embellished his

THE WAY BROTHER JONATHAN WILL ASTONISH THE NATIVES.

ANNEXATION COMES IN BY THE RAIL, WHILE LIBERTY FLIES OFF IN THE SMOKE.

A sinister looking Brother Jonathan (the pre-Uncle Sam depiction of the U.S.) comes barreling down the track, crushing an unwary Canadian. Punch's *cartoon sounded a weighty warning to those who courted the notion that union with the U.S. was the solution to Canada's problems.*

regal manor, Dundurn Castle perched on Burlington Heights overlooking Lake Ontario, and plunged wildly ahead with plans for his Great Western Railway, A.T. Galt was at work peopling the Eastern Townships of Lower Canada with solid Britishers and sprinkling the territory with the seeds of the St. Lawrence and Atlantic Railway.

Galt became obsessed with the need to connect the interior and Montreal with an all-weather port on the Atlantic seaboard. Boston was the obvious choice, but the ambitious Maine railway promoter, John A. Poor, lobbied convincingly for Portland, Maine, 280 miles from Montreal. Galt and his colleagues agreed. The Canadian parliament incorporated the St. Lawrence and Atlantic Railway in 1845 and empowered it to build a line to the New Hampshire border where it was to join the line running down to Portland. The latter half was chartered by the states of Maine and New Hampshire.

a nose for money

With his neat genius for organization and trained nose for money, Galt set out to muster the capital for the Canadian half of the railway. But Canadians were reluctant to invest. Between Montreal and the Townships, Galt raised but £100,000 – about one-fifth the required amount. England was in the throws of railroad mania and Galt sailed for London to appeal for pounds sterling. Close behind followed Allan MacNab, pursuing still his Great Western dream.

After a brief flurry of interest, efforts by both men failed and they returned to begin again a long and dreary appeal to Canadian investors. It was perhaps the only time in history that railway shares were purchased with butter, eggs and meat. Farmers in the Townships took shares in return for produce used to feed the construction gangs.

Unable to entice sufficient Canadian capital, Galt and his directors in the end fell back on government aid, setting an indelible pattern for financing Canadian railroads. The time was ripe. Men like Hincks, then inspector-general of U.C., and John A. Macdonald, an influential politician, were receptive. MacNab, a member of the assembly himself, was champing to win aid for his schemes, and so it was a natural marriage when MacNab and Galt joined forces in the House.

the speculator's dream

With their help, Francis Hincks was able to push through parliament the Guarantee Act of 1849, by which the government guaranteed payment of six per cent interest on bonds of any railway over seventy-five miles long. The act assured potential investors of a return on their money even before the line was completed, fueling the fires of overbuilding and speculative prompting.

Hincks and friends followed with the Municipal Loan Act of 1852, to provide provincial credit for municipalities to construct local lines. When the bust came in 1857, many towns and municipalities which had borrowed over six and a half million dollars, collapsed in financial ruin with but a few miles of rusting iron for their trouble. The failure of the Bank of Upper Canada a few years later is attributed to the misuse of public funds in politicians' railway schemes during the boom.

Despite setbacks, Galt's St. Lawrence and Atlantic began to take shape. By December 7, 1948 thirty miles of track connected St.-Hyacinthe and Longueil. Montreal merchants, bedevilled by ice-bound merchandise, started to see the light. Before the line to Portland could be completed however, an even grander vision appeared before the Canadian legislators. First called merely the Main Trunk Line, it came to be known as The Grand Trunk Railway. It eventually linked Quebec City,

A dozen shady characters and one dandy (sporting white spats and top hat) are hanging around Niagara Falls' Clifton Station, wondering when the next Great Western train is due to chug in.

71

The earliest wire-cable suspension bridge in Canada was built in 1851-55 across the Niagara River, a span of 851 feet. Its designer, John Roebling, gained world renown 30 years later with New York's famous Brooklyn Bridge.

Jokingly called the "Oats, Straw and Hay Railway," the Ontario, Simcoe and Huron was the brainchild of Frederick Chase Capreol of Toronto. In 1849, "Mad Capreol" concocted the idea of a $2 million lottery to finance the project, with shares in the company to the winners. City fathers turned thumbs down on the idea, and Capreol was turfed out before a mile of track was laid.

Montreal, Toronto and Michigan.

As each section of the Grand Trunk was completed a civic carnival marked the triumph. On October 27, 1856, when service between Toronto and Montreal was officially opened, a historic train ride on the "Celebration Special" was followed by three days of jollification which cost the Montreal public £10,000. All along the line, crowds gathered to cheer the train although according to one witness it was not the *smoothest* ride in the history of transportation.

Woodburning locomotives produced plumes of smoke and clouds of dust as passengers jostled and choked in the cramped carriages. After the fourteen hour ride – $10 first class, $8 second class – the travellers were still enthusiastic for the revelries in Montreal. The first banquet was held in the Grand Trunk's workshop at Point St. Charles, an elaborate affair described in the Montreal *Gazette*:

We need hardly state that the building was fitted up with great taste. There were seventy-four dining tables (exclusive of side tables), covered with 1,500 yards or nearly a mile of table cloth! On these tables were 44,000 knives and forks and an equal number of spoons, tumblers and wine glasses. The line of space occupied by the guests was 8,000 feet or about a mile and three-quarters. The chair was occupied by H. Starnes, Esq., Mayor of Montreal and on his right was His Excellency the Governor-General. . . . In the evening there was a torchlight procession and other illuminations.

On the second day the crush at the Grand Ball was so great that the ladies' fashionable hoops suffered considerably. Between seven and eight thousand made merry and dancing did not commence in earnest until one o'clock in the morning because the room was too crowded to permit it.

72

Construction on the Grand Trunk Railway's Victoria Bridge at Montreal began in 1854, with the building of 24 stone piers, anchored to the river bottom from floating dams. Over 3,000 men worked on the mammoth project for five years.

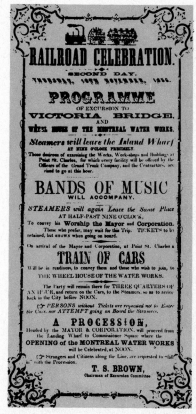

Three days of non-stop partying signalled the completion of the Toronto-to-Montreal stretch of the Grand Trunk Railway. On the programme for the second day of celebrations was an excursion by steamer to the Victoria Bridge construction site. Considered by some the "world's eighth wonder," the bridge was designed by Robert Stephenson, son of the inventor of the steam locomotive, and the line's chief engineer, A. M. Ross.

On the third day, after visitors steamboated on the St. Lawrence to view the Victoria Bridge, then under construction by the Grand Trunk, they entrained to visit Montreal's new waterworks and were treated to a brisk military review on the Champ de Mars. They witnessed a display of fireworks along the waterfront that confounded them with Maltese Crosses, palm trees, shells, civic shields and the insignia of the Mechanics' Institute, nothing less than an "uplifted arm, hammer, etc. decorated with a beautiful green wreath in imitation of Nature."

The Grand Trunk Railway Company of Canada was chartered in 1852 with a capitalization of £3,000,000, which eventually climbed to £12,000,000. By 1855, the company was too impoverished to continue construction and floated a loan from the government for £9,000,000, which it failed to pay back. In the end, the government of Canada contributed £3,111,500 to the railroad. Its wild and glorious speculation led to "a failure so magnificent, complete and disastrous" that violent accusations hounded almost every person in any way connected with the folly. But the railway was built, and perhaps that was the most important thing.

Small railways were blooming like roses all over Canada by the mid-fifties. Each new stretch was hailed as a social and historical event. The Peterborough-Cobourg Railway was short but it was long aborning–twenty years. The original charter was granted in 1834 and on Friday, December 29, 1854, one thousand eager travellers filled twelve carriages to make the first railroad journey from Cobourg on Lake Ontario, north to Peterborough.

They set out at a speed of fifteen miles per hour (allowing one of the doubters to walk to the celebration and still arrive in time for dinner). To

Proud as punch, Grand Trunk officials and trainmen pose beside No. 162, one of 50 gleaming red, green and black Birkenhead locomotives built in England (1854-58). Besides those built in their own shops, the GTR *bought 10 magnificent engines from Montreal's Kinmond Bros., and others from the U.S. and Scotland.*

stress the day's importance, Peterborough was aglow with triumphal arches and colourful banners. The town fathers had invited the directors of the railroad and fifty other distinguished gentlemen to dine on fresh cod from Boston, venison from the backwoods and various costly wines.

Later journeys on the railroad proved to be dangerous, however, due to the shaky structure of the Rice Lake Bridge. It was soon considered so unstable that a man followed each train on a hand-car and checked out every beam and bolt. In 1860, when HRH Prince of Wales paid his memorable visit to Canada, he was invited to detrain at Rice Lake and cross the water by boat. A passenger on the last train run by the Peterborough-Cobourg recalled that the bridge swayed so much he thought his end had come.

never-ending repair bills

Labourers on the ill-fated line – it was not to survive the never-ending repair bills to bridge and track that piled on its initial million dollar cost – were paid a whopping dollar a day. In an age of almost daily railroading inventions, they were luckier than their predecessors who laid the "snake rails," wooden tracks topped with flat iron that curled up in the summer sun. Passengers, like those on the Cobourg line paying a dollar for the jolting, smokey trip, were appeased somewhat by the announcement of dazzling 1858 innovations such as Braid's Spark Arrester, Egan's Car Journal Oiler, Hudson's Fastener for Car Seats, Webster's Improved Car Link and Draw Car, Fox's Apparatus for Railroad Switching, McDonald's Improved Axle Box and especially Crawford's Machine for Arresting Railway Trains.

The hazard of early train travel in the Canadas wasn't immortalized in song as it was in the United States. But the trials of the thousands of souls who boarded the trains for a taste of this novel, bone-rattling experience were equally worthy of notes. On jaunts short and long, they were taking their lives into their hands.

In 1854, there were nineteen serious accidents on the Great Western alone, climaxing in a collision killing fifty-two and injuring forty-eight.

maniacal crews

Train crews were both unskilled and maniacal; they drove trains to suit themselves. Power-madness seized engineers like a virulent fever, and they put themselves out to knock down stray cows, herd passengers into freight cars, take paying customers past their destinations and even assault those who dared complain. Maintenance crews were whimsical to the point of insanity – leaving water tanks empty, wood storage bins bare and sections of rail at loose ends. Signals were misunderstood and sometimes ignored.

The first train robbery attempt occurred on the Great Western, too. In what sounds like an early movie serial, two unidentified brigands tore up a piece of track near London, UC, with the idea of derailing the train and looting it. An alert track inspector, making his rounds that night, happened upon the vandals and was shot for his trouble. He still managed to hike back to the station and warn the coming train. The saboteurs though foiled, were never caught.

The unscheduled perils and adventures that awaited unsuspecting travellers were painstakingly chronicled by one young man who braved the purchase of a ticket on the Grand Trunk.

Myles Pennington, an official in the shipping end of the railroad business, was a meticulous diary-keeper. Early one March he set out by train from Montreal to Toronto in an attempt to "slip through between snowstorms".

The journey got off to a bad start . . . six hours late. When the sleeping cars were finally made up,

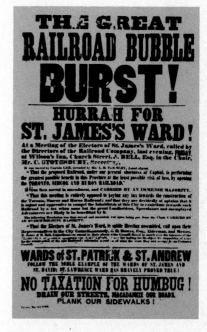

Toronto taxpayers tried to pop the "great railway bubble" with this protest meeting in 1850. At a time when most workers still felt the grip of depression on their pocketbooks, why should they pay for a railway (the Ontario, Simcoe and Huron) that would benefit "none but the great Landholders, Speculators and unemployed Adventurers!" Humbug! "Drain our streets, macadamize our roads and plank our sidewalks, instead," screamed their poster.

**Allan MacNab
The Great Western's Tory**

"Intriguing, slippery, unprincipled" was how Governor General Bagot described MacNab. Harsh words? Perhaps, but fitting the brash, old-line Tory who sparked some of the era's hottest political battles. He was a born "scrapper": at 15 the "Boy Hero" of his regiment in the War of 1812; leader of the loyal "Men of Gore" in 1837; and arch-defender of "family compact" power after his 1841 election to the Canadian assembly. His unbridled tongue nearly led to a fist-fight in Parliament in 1849, when he branded French-Canadians "rebels and aliens." Much-mellowed, he headed the government in 1854 and 1856, but his term was short-lived. Plagued by gout, his judgement on railway issues impaired (he was the president of the Great Western), and strained by debts on Dundurn Castle, his Hamilton mansion, he was forced to resign when his cabinet deserted.

Pennington noted his pleasure at being able to "creep under nice clean sheets." However, all was not well. Soon one hundred and fifty passengers were locked together in chilly adventure when the train ground to a halt three miles east of Gananoque.

An auxiliary engine failed to move the train through the snow and the passengers were abandoned by their own engine when it chugged off to Gananoque for relief. By noon they were without sustenance and heat. The passengers rummaged through their bags for bits of food.

"One musters a few sandwiches," Pennington reported, "another a few apples or an orange or a few crackers." Another man accompanied by two children produced a food basket which yielded two bottles of milk, sandwiches, ginger cakes and candies. The loot was divided among all passengers. "Deep in the recesses of his carpet-bag one old gentleman finds an ancient meat pie." Though somewhat dry, it was pronounced excellent.

Hours went by. A hardy fellow decided to venture to the nearest farmhouse through the blinding snow. One can almost hear the cheering as he appeared again, "a spectral object," carrying a bundle of food and a jug of hot tea. Expeditions to nearby farmhouses were then undertaken by several passengers, and settlers willingly cooked and offered food to the stranded travellers.

At 2:00 AM the next morning, the snow was still falling. Some passengers managed to sleep but the "air is close and sickly, the lamps cast a yellow light upon the upturned faces seen below."

frosty poetry

Twenty yards ahead loomed the dark outline of the stalled locomotive which had tried to rescue the train. Here Pennington waxed poetic. "The snow has held high revel under it, on it, and around it, adding many a piece of ornamental

frost-work to its iron sides."

The snow had reached the platforms of the cars when a gang of workers arrived in the morning to dig out the train. Soon sleigh bells were heard and provisions arrived: steaming hot coffee, thick sandwiches, and a general feeling of *bonhomie* among the stranded. Three whistles signalled the arrival of three engines and a snowplough. Finally, the little train was released and on its way again. The Grand Trunk, Pennington noted, provided a free dinner for all.

Toronto in sixty-two hours

But the escapade was not quite over. Everything went well until 2:00 AM the next day when the train once again shuddered to a halt. An eastbound train blocked the way. Passengers bundled in rugs and heavy coats proceeded single file through deep snow to exchange places on the two trains. The eastbound train then backed westbound with its new travellers and the westbound reversed in an easterly direction. Pennington and his fellow adventurers backed into the Toronto station a full sixty-two hours after leaving Montreal.

The Grand Trunk was destined to disappear into the great maw of a national railroad, but in 1861, despite early chaos, intermittent ignorance and the occasional touch of bliss, the Grand Trunk averaged 84,832 passenger miles each day. It owned 88 first class passenger cars, 45 second class passenger cars and 223 locomotives. By 1870 its line extended from Portland, Maine, to Detroit, Michigan, a distance of 854 miles. With the addition of branch lines, the Grand Trunk had laid 1,377 miles of track.

Perhaps rail travel was iffy at times, dangerous at others, but it was not without its moments. Whatever the price, the Iron Horse had arrived, and if not always on time, it seemed to work.

The Iron Horse

The "iron horse" made its Canada West debut in October 1852 with the arrival of the Ontario, Simcoe & Huron Railway's first locomotive, the *Lady Elgin*. Built by a firm in Portland, Maine, it was a crude piece of machinery compared with the elegant engines being made for other lines at the time. In fact, six months later, when the *Toronto* rolled out of James Good's foundry on Front Street, the frumpy *Lady Elgin* was demoted to construction duty, and the new engine made the line's maiden run from Toronto to Machell's Corners (now Aurora, Ontario). In many ways, the "Oats, Straw and Hay Railway" was typical of early railroads in the country. Chartered in 1834, years of "talking, surveying, scheming, sleeping and issuing prospectuses" passed before the sod turning ceremony in 1851. Even then there was no end to problems. Disputes flared over who should pay the tab and where stations should be erected. On the first test run, one car derailed and plunged down a sharp embankment. But the line was completed to Hen and Chickens Harbour (renamed Collingwood) in 1855, and prosperity followed its route north to Lake Huron's Georgian Bay.

The Toronto Patriot *heralded the arrival of the* Lady Elgin *(above) with* HURRAH FOR THE NORTH, *and warned owls, bats, wolves and bears* en route *to run for cover.*

Ontario, Simcoe and Huron ticket offices proudly put up hand-painted posters (right) advertising their stretch of the "Great Northern & Western Route through Canada."

From Horsepower to Steam

With the advent of practical steam engines in the first decades of the 19th century, a new era of technology was born, and the burden of work for people and animals became lighter. By mid-century, the fate of the great Maritime sailing ships was written on the wind, as one after another of Samuel Cunard's steamers puffed into port. Regular steamer service on the St. Lawrence and the Great Lakes spelled the end to *bateaux*, Durham boats and horse-ferries, and the coming of the "iron horse" eliminated stage-coach travel between most major towns and cities. Steam shovels were already in use in the U.S., and steam rollers in France. Look out, Dobbin.

Caroline Walker, later an art teacher at Bishop Strachan School in Toronto, took an unusual interest (for a woman of her time) in industry and technology. From the late-1850s to the early-1870s, she sketched oil wells in operation at Bothwell and pick-and-shovel strip mining at Marmora's Gatling Gold Mine (above)

An anonymous artist sketched this scene on the St. Lawrence River at the Long Sault near Cornwall, showing vestiges of the past—the timber raft, the canoe and the Durham boat (background)—and three two-stacked steamers. The steamboat at the left is just passing through the Cornwall Canal, completed in 1843.

Looking more like the legendary American hero
Davy Crockett than the Irish landowner's son
that he was, John Palliser had already spent
a year in the North American wilds before he
proposed his plan for surveying the Canadian
West to the Royal Geographical Society. Like
his five brothers (two had hunted big game in
Ceylon, one had rescued a lady from pirates in
China, another had crossed the Australian out-
back, and the fifth had died in the Arctic on
Franklin's last expedition), the 39-year-old
bachelor had grappled with grizzlies and run
buffalo on the American Plains in 1847. An
ardent sportsman and crack marksman, the big,
burly Irishman was fluent in five languages
and once sang both the bass and tenor parts in
a concert performance of the oratorio David.

CHAPTER SEVEN

Westward Ho!

There is a spot on this continent which travellers do not visit and from which civilization seems in a measure shut out. No railroads, or steamers, or telegraph wires, or lines of stages make their way thither . . . no paragraph in any newspaper records its weal or woe. . . .

"The Red River Settlement," *Harper's,* 1856

Almost all the vast Northwest, from the Great Lakes, across the Prairies, through the Rockies and down the coastal slope to the Pacific, was charted in the mid-nineteenth century.

Millions of acres had never been touched by man – white or Indian – and no one in the British government or the parliament of the Province of Canada really knew whether the land could be tamed. Could British and European colonists endure the harsh winters and grow crops? Were there valuable natural resources? Equally important, would it be practical to build useable roads and forge rail lines around the forbidding north shore of Lake Superior and across the prairies?

Fortunately, a handful of enterprising men appeared to unveil some of the mysteries. Between 1855 and 1861, expeditions headed by British officers, with sextants and cameras; American deputations, laden with heavy equipment; and less official groups, led by dashing adventurers, tough-

minded doctors and finicky botanists, trekked across the western landscape. By the time the calendar turned to 1860, the Lake of the Woods country was mapped, the two Saskatchewan Rivers were charted, new mountain passes were revealed and the boundary between British and American territory was marked from the edge of the Pacific to the foothills of the Rockies.

Of all the men who made vital contributions, the most colourful was Captain John Palliser of the Waterford Militia. He came from a distinguished Irish landowning family: Protestant, conservative, six generations removed from influential Yorkshire stock (one of his ancestors was an archbishop).

On a private hunt in Arkansas Territory in 1847, Palliser fell in love with the great continental plains where he brought down a splendid panther, wrestled a bear with four-inch claws and was tossed on the horns of a bull buffalo. The experience excited him so much that he was determined to return as soon as possible.

Slaughtering dangerous animals came almost naturally to the landed gentry, and given a worthy beast to pot at, the upper class Britisher was more than happy to oblige. So in 1853, when the thirty-six-year-old Palliser published his breathtaking account of the Arkansas expedition, *Solitary Rambles and Adventures of a Hunter in the Prairies,* he became an instant idol of his set.

The first book printed in the West was not in English or French but in a strange, "hieroglyphic" alphabet invented by missionary James Evans to represent the sounds of the Cree dialect. This is one page from the 16-page hymnary Evans printed in 1841 at the HBC *post, Norway House.*

The "country wife" (left) of one of the HBC fur traders watches the work at the Company post. Most traders and officials kept native women as helpmates and wives à la façon du pays.

But Palliser's family fortunes had dwindled by the early 1850's and he could no longer afford the role of great white hunter. With his usual panache he touted a survey of British North American prairieland to the Royal Geographic Society in London. Naturally, he hoped for financial backing. Palliser's original concept was somewhat naive: a personal odyssey embellished from time to time with just enough scientific morsels to keep the geographers happy.

He was a crack shot, a painfully honest accountant and a soaring optimist. His fellow explorers were, like the game they subsequently killed, a mixed bag. Eugene Bourgeau was forty-four, a botanist who spoke no English but was a careful cataloguist of flora and fauna. Twenty-four-year-old Lieutenant Thomas Blakiston was a disenchanted, irascible artillery officer who had served with distinction in the Crimea but a naturalist by inclination. Doctor James Hector was a like-minded hunter with the stamina of an ox and the disposition of a saint who had only briefly practised medicine. He was twenty-three. Finally, there was John William Sullivan, twenty-one, astronomer and secretary to Palliser.

the threefold mandate

Palliser's mandate was threefold: examine the country between the Great Lakes and the Red River, chart it and report on vegetation, rivers and inhabitants; survey the southern prairies from the Assiniboine River to the headwaters of the South Saskatchewan; and explore the Rocky Mountains in search of an access south of the Athabasca Pass.

Palliser and his group reached the Red River settlement in July, 1857. It lay about forty miles south of Lake Winnipeg, sprawling between the forks of the Red and Assiniboine Rivers. The settlement was an island in an earth-stream: cut off from Canada West and the populated east by the craggy swamp-land of the Great Lakes country and equally isolated from Pacific trading posts by miles of flatland and the Rockies.

each to his own

When Palliser and his expedition arrived, there were 1,082 families at Red River, five hundred of whom were Indian-European Métis living above the forks of the two rivers. The races tended to segregate, for Europeans held land between the two Fort Garrys while the Métis settlement squatted lower down the river. Less than half the Métis males farmed; the rest were carefree hunters who relied on buffalo meat and selling furs to see them through the bitter western winters. Lieutenant Blakiston observed:

Red River Settlement is neither a city, town or even a village, but, as the name indicates, a settlement consisting of a straggling chain of small farm establishments, extending for a distance of forty miles along the banks, but mostly on the west bank of the Red River of the North, the dwellings being from fifty yards to a mile apart, while at intervals along this line are a few churches and windmills, besides two establishments of the Hudson's Bay Company, built in the form of forts, one at the junction of the Assiniboine with the main river, and the other twenty miles below. On the north bank of the Assiniboine also, which has a general east course, the settlement extends about 25 miles up, and about 50 miles further is another small collection of homesteads, usually called the Portage.

The valley's soil was rich. Farmers harvested forty bushels of wheat to the acre and grew oats, barley, Indian corn, potatoes, turnips, peas, cabbage, rhubarb, radishes, mangels, carrots, hops, pumpkins and melons. Nearby swamps provided excellent hay for livestock. Every man was his own butter and cheesemaker, tanner, carpenter and mason. He also distilled his own whisky and brewed his own beer. Women wove cloth, baked, gardened and made sugar from the ubiquitous maple. Salt was skimmed from Lake Manitoba. But despite what seemed like a bottomless cornucopia, a large quantity of dry goods, farm implements and food staples had to be imported by the HBC via York Fort on Hudson Bay or brought by boat and cart from St. Paul across the U.S. border.

There was no mail service. The HBC carried personal letters by boat along the northern route, or private travellers took them first to Fort Pembina, just across the border and from there to St. Paul.

Beyond the settlement paper money and coins were rarely used – men were paid in coats, trousers, guns, ammunition, blankets, tobacco or tools.

a wretched summation

As the expedition prepared to leave Red River, Palliser summed up the colony as half-developed, a place where the people were lazy and serious farmers handicapped by lack of labourers. The reason, he wrote, was that the Métis were "child-like. They hunt three months of the year, beg, borrow and starve the remaining time."

In late July, Palliser sent part of his expedition west with supplies and horses while he detoured south to Pembina below the border with twelve men and thirty horses. Palliser and his group reached Souris River on August 20. By mid-September they reached Qu'Appelle Lake in what is now southern Saskatchewan. There they visited an HBC post and Assiniboine Indians cultivating corn, barley and potatoes.

The expedition reached Moose Jaw Creek in late September, deep in the heart of buffalo country. Cree and Blackfoot tribes warred constantly over horse-stealing, and the vast plain was a buffer zone. Neither tribe would enter the area without

George Simpson
The Little Emperor

The only thing little about the man they called the "Little Emperor" was his stature – 5'4". In every other way, George Simpson was one of the "biggest" men in the business world of his day. As governor of the HBC's North American empire for 40 years, he controlled more territory and money than the petty potentates of Europe put together. Three times he crossed the continent in his big, brightly-coloured, nine-man *canot du nord*, always accompanied by his Highland piper and a "negro cook." Born out-of-wedlock in Scotland in 1787, he worked 10 years as a sugar broker's clerk before being named governor of the HBC in 1820 at 33. A master of efficiency, he quickly consolidated the Nor'Westers' and the Hudson's Bay's operations, and personally supervised all areas of the trade. Besides his five children by marriage to his cousin, Frances, he had many others by "country wives."

**John Rowand
Lord of Edmonton's Folly**

Fur traders passing through Fort Edmonton called the big, sprawling, three-storey house on the bluffs "Rowand's Folly," but its builder knew the huge rooms, paintings and sculptures, and real glass windows (the first in the West) would awe his Indian trappers. John Rowand knew them well. When he first came west as a North West Company clerk at 17 in 1804, a Blackfoot woman saved his life, and he took her as his wife. He had survived tribal wars and epidemics (the worst in 1837 – smallpox – killed two-thirds of the Blackfoot Nation). Above all, he was a shrewd trader, a man after George Simpson's own heart. In fact, in 1841, he accompanied the "Little Emperor" to Honolulu on the Governor's round-the-world tour. And when Rowand died at 65, Simpson had his bones dug up and buried at the Montreal family plot.

The three men repairing the canoe for the trip to Red River in 1846 must have been quicker than Hampden Moody of the Royal Engineers expected: the gent's umbrella and the Métis chef's cooking tripod and pot are barely pencilled in.

knowing of the other's whereabouts. Buffalo apparently enjoyed the uneasy truce as Palliser observed:

The whole region as far as the eye could reach was covered with buffalo, in bands varying from hundreds to thousands. So vast were the herds that I began to have serious apprehensions for my horses as the grass was eaten to the earth.

When winter settled in, Palliser's group was at Fort Carlton on the North Saskatchewan River. He left men, horses and supplies at the fort while he returned to Montreal through Minnesota to transmit the expedition's report on Indians, climate, rivers and vegetation to the Colonial Office in London.

June of 1858 found Palliser back at Fort Carlton ready to push westward toward the forks of the Red Deer and Medicine Rivers. His trials dur-

ing this second summer season made his first exploration look like a stroll through a woodland glade; but his spirits remained high. When the expedition's supplies were reduced to nothing but tea, he figured the beverage would be useful against possible cases of dysentery from drinking swamp water. When they were out of firewood, he cheerfully discovered that buffalo dung made a good cooking fire.

Food packs were empty again on June 24, but the party "fell in with a band of buffalo" and they ate once more. Shortly afterwards he had tied his best horse to the horns of a dead buffalo he had been skinning and the animal worked loose and ran off. Mounting an inferior horse, Palliser pushed the expedition on to the Battle River. They reached it on July 7, mapping the territory and cataloguing vegetation and animal life as they went. Palliser expressed naive irritation:

Four independent (and often squabbling) settlements with a total population of 5,000 clustered near the Forks of Red River: Scottish, French and Métis, English, and HBC officers headquartered at Lower and Upper Fort Garry (above).

**Isobel Finlayson
A Trader's Wife**

Unfortunately, the Indians have a disastrous habit of setting the prairie on fire for the most trivial reasons.

While it appeared that way to Palliser, Plains Indians skillfully set ground fires to corral game and for defense or attack in war.

Undaunted by famine, fire or flood, Palliser and his men pushed west. Lieutenant Balkiston had taken a side-trip to Fort Edmonton to get tea, sugar, cereal and other much-needed supplies. When he rejoined Palliser he brought no food as the supply boats had not reached Fort Edmonton. Palliser was philosophical, however. "He has brought ammunition, the only thing of vital importance."

The party's collective heart was soon warmed by the distant tramp of buffalo hooves, and between them the men brought down sixteen animals. But with Palliser adversity could not be far

off. When the expedition reached the Rockies, elk and deer were scarce, and to add to his difficulties, Palliser had a falling out with Blakiston over the appointment of Dr. Hector as second-in-command. Blakiston stalked off, taking ten horses, an Indian guide and three men to investigate two passes to the south which might lead to the Kootenay River. It was a permanent split. Blakiston turned in an excellent individual report when he returned to London and charted two useable passes through the Rockies.

Dr. Hector, naturalist-geologist, stuck with Palliser. They were much alike in spirit, and Hector's escapades while on separate jaunts in the Rocky Mountains ran a close second to Palliser's own. It is due to one of Hector's misfortunes that Kicking Horse Pass got its name:

Here I received a severe kick in the chest from my

In the fur trade it was no secret, but to proper, young ladies like Isobel Finlayson it must have come as a shock to learn that there were children in the country who called their husbands "daddy." Sister of Frances Simpson (the wife of HBC Governor George Simpson), Isobel arrived at Fort Garry in 1839 as the pretty, young wife of Duncan Finlayson, the new governor of Assiniboia. Her husband had been in the fur trade since 1815, first as a trader, then as chief factor of the Saskatchewan District. No doubt he too (like Simpson, John McTavish, William Connolly and a host of other company officials) had at least one "country wife." Indeed, Isobel may well have heard of such goings-on from her sister in 1833, when Frances returned to London after three wretched years. By 1859, Isobel was back home, too.

Hime's portrait of the expedition's Scottish-Cree interpreter, John McKay, is among the 47 photos that survived the journey. The building is part of the original Selkirk settlement.

H. L. Hime, Photographer

Some of the other men on the Assiniboine and Saskatchewan Exploring Expedition of 1858 must have thought Humphrey Lloyd Hime was crazy—lugging around his huge box camera, tripod, lenses, case-load of fragile glass plates, chemicals, scales, graduated cylinders, rinsing pail, black sheets and what-not. Studio portraits were one thing (okay for those vain people who wanted to look at themselves all the time), but this was carrying photography a bit too far! And sure enough, it was. Before Hime, not one photograph had been snapped on the Canadian prairies. In fact, the leader of the 1858 expedition, Henry Youle Hind (see page 88) wasn't taking chances: he brought along artist John Fleming, just in case. West of Red River, the party was plagued by locusts and wet weather, and only eight of Hime's photos have survived. But back at the site of present—day Winnipeg, the photographer met with more success and made some three dozen negatives, many of them sold to the *Illustrated London News* and later reproduced as a portfolio of 30 prints. Photographer and civil engineer Hime returned to his firm in Toronto after the journey, turned his energies to real estate, and became a founder, and later the president, of the Toronto Stock Exchange.

Possibly the first photograph taken in the West, Humphrey Lloyd Hime caught the members of the Assiniboine and Saskatchewan Exploring Expedition at camp beside their long canoe on June 1, 1848. The man at the centre, sitting on a crate, looks like Henry Youle Hind, leader of the survey party.

**Henry Youle Hind
The Professor**

Chemist, geologist, writer, editor, university professor, explorer – Henry Youle Hind's interests and abilities seemed limitless. Coming to Canada in 1846 at age 23, he taught at Toronto's Normal School and Trinity College before tiring of academia. In 1857, he headed a government geological expedition to Red River; a year later, he trekked further west with the Assiniboine and Saskatchewan Exploring group. In 1861, he and his brother, artist William Hind, explored Labrador; in 1864, he surveyed New Brunswick; in 1867, Nova Scotia's goldfields. In short, by the time Hind retired, he knew more about what was above, on and under most areas of Canada than most people really wanted to know – at least during his lifetime. The generation after his death in 1908 gave new meaning to "resources."

horse rendering me senseless and disabling me for some time. My recovery might have been more tedious than it was but for the fact that we were now starving and I found it necessary to push on.

Only the blink of his eye, which was all Hector could manage, saved the doctor from an unspeakable end. His men were about to bury him alive.

In October, 1858, Palliser's expedition was in the Fort Colville area in the Rocky Mountains. They met up with a surveying party from the boundary commission sent out by the United States to mark the line between British and American territory on the west coast and over the mountains.

In his journal, dated October 11, 1858, Palliser reported:

A little further on I came in sight of the observatory, containing the zenith telescope, used by the Commission for laying down the boundary line. On riding into their camp I was most hospitably received by the scientific gentlemen employed on the survey, and invited to pass the day with them, an invitation which I gladly availed myself of. There are three parties on the American boundary survey; each party consists of an observer, computer, and topographer, protected by an officer and company of regular soldiers.

Palliser's report on his expedition was detailed and, in general, encouraged settlement. He described "Palliser's Triangle" as an area not suited to farming due to uncertain rainfall, lack of water and timber. Roughly, the triangle encompassed the southwestern prairies from a point south of what is now Brandon, Manitoba; north west above the South Saskatchewan River to the foothills near the present site of Calgary, Alberta; its base being the American border.

Palliser described land along the North Saskatchewan River and in the Red River Valley itself, as fertile, farming practical. As for a railroad, he was negative about construction around the north shore of Lake Superior, in British territory. He felt the section should run along the south shores of the Great Lakes in American territory, re-entering British territory north of Fort Pembina.

While Palliser was making his historic journeys, another expedition commissioned by the Province of Canada, was making its assessment. Headed by Henry Youle Hind and Simon Dawson, the party set out for the west in 1857. Hind visualized a dam at the elbow of the South Saskatchewan River to divert water down the Qu'Appelle Valley and provide a water route between the foothills and the Red River settlement. Hind was more optimistic about a railway through all-British territory than Palliser. However, he agreed with Palliser that the entire North Saskatchewan Valley was fertile country and that an arid belt, roughly comparable to Palliser's Triangle, was unfit for human habitation.

Palliser summed up his expedition:

The territory which has now been examined and mapped by this expedition ranges from Lake Superior to the eastern shore of the lesser Oakanagan Lake, and from the boundary line to the water shed of the Arctic Ocean. This large belt of country embraces districts, some of which are valuable for the purposes of agriculturists, while others will forever be comparatively useless.

In the end, Palliser's report, combining the work of all members of the expedition, suggested so strongly that the western plains be settled, that it helped persuade a reluctant and somewhat ignorant British government to take a hard line with the mighty Hudson's Bay Company. The land *would* be peopled and farmed one day as part of Canada.

At the same time that John Palliser and Henry Youle Hind were exploring parts of the West, a hundred British Royal Engineers were establishing the 49th parallel boundary with the U.S. Above, Captain R. E. Darrah (standing) and a junior astronomer man the zenith telescope at the Yahk River (B.C.) station.

The Old West

Though still very much the private domain of Hudson's Bay Company traders and native tribes, the West – at least the "Old West" from Fort William to Red River – became the focus of Canada's interest after the first pioneer-half of the 19th century. Inter-marriages and small-scale immigration were creating self-sufficient pocket-colonies around some company forts, noticeably around Fort Garry. With the U.S. moving vigorously westward, Canada would have to keep pace.

Artist-spy Lt. Henry Warre crossed the country in 1845, and (in the guise of a foot-loose sportsman) made a reconnaissance of U.S. strength along the yet-undefined border. At Old Fort Garry (above), HBC *Governor George Simpson persuaded him that a garrison there would deter a U.S. move northward.*

Artist William Napier accompanied Henry Youle Hind's 1857 Canadian Government Expedition to Red River, with a stop-over at Fort William (above). Once the famous French fur fort, Kaministikwia, and from 1801-21 the North West Company's Lakehead depot, the fort regained importance with western expansion.

CHAPTER EIGHT

Uncle Tom

Pass him on! Pass him on!
Another soul from slavery won;
Another man erect *to stand*
Fearless of the scourge and brand.

H.G. Adams, "A Lay of the Under-Ground Railroad"

Josiah Henson's gruelling march from the slave state of Kentucky to freedom on the Canadian side of the Niagara River was typical of thousands of escapes by American Blacks between 1830 and 1860. Twenty years later, Henson was prospering as the hero of Harriet Beecher Stowe's bestselling novel, *Uncle Tom's Cabin,* but on the moonless September night when he first ran away from his owner, Henson feared for his life. He had a small parcel of food, twenty-five cents, the clothes on his back, his frail wife and four young children.

The Hensons crossed the Ohio River in a skiff, with the two youngest children in a sack on his back. The state of Ohio, on the far bank was free but not without slave-hunters. Henson had been told he would find friends to conduct him to Canada on the "Underground Railroad" and he put his trust in that.

Two days walk from Cincinnati Henson and his family ran out of food, but once they reached that community, sympathizers took them in, fed them and steered them north toward Canada. They travelled thirty miles in a wagon and after that first comfortable lift, tramped by night

through the bush and rested by day until they found an old military trail cut by General Hull during the War of 1812.

No one told Henson that they would be travelling through wilderness, and he neglected to bring much food. Soon hungry once again and worried by wolves (they could hear them howling during the night), they subsisted on a bit of dried beef. On the second day, Henson's wife collapsed. A party of Indians finally rescued them and gave them shelter.

When they reached Sandusky on the shore of Lake Erie, Henson spotted a vessel being loaded and was hired for the day. Captain Burnham, a gruff Scot, offered to transport the Henson family along the lake to Buffalo. Within a day they reached Black Rock and the captain paid their passage on a ferry and gave Henson an extra dollar. On the October 28, 1830, Henson threw himself down on Canadian soil. They had reached the end of the Underground Railroad.

Underground Railroad was a somewhat fanciful name for a very much above-ground network of northern United States' homes and people sympathetic to the slaves' plight. It stretched from the banks of the Ohio near Cincinnati to Windsor, Amherstburg, Chatham and Dresden in Canada West, and through Vermont to Canada East.

According to one of the "conductors" on the railroad, Reverend W.M. Mitchell, a Black, the

Uncle Tom's Cabin *may not have sparked America's Civil War (as Lincoln once quipped), but it did assure Josiah Henson, the Canadian ex-slave on whose life the author based parts of the book, of life-long fame as the "real Uncle Tom."*

Opposite page: *This extraordinary painting of Uncle Tom and Little Eva by Ira Barton (and its more extraordinary snail-shell frame) now hang at Upper Canada Village. Appropriate, considering the many thousands of fugitive slaves who fled to Canada from 1840 to 1860.*

**Josiah Henson
The Man and the Myth**

Three years before Harriet Beecher Stowe rocked the U.S. with *Uncle Tom's Cabin,* a 76-page pamphlet was published by the Anti-Slavery Society of Boston. Mrs. Stowe, an active abolitionist, certainly read it (as she did the dozens of other anti-slavery tracts printed by New England presses at the time), but most of the parallels between her Uncle Tom and Josiah Henson have to be read between the lines. True, Aunt Chloe, Topsy, Little Eva and Eliza are recognizable as Henson's wife and other slaves on the Amos Riley farm where Josiah worked as overseer, but there was nothing of the "Yes, mas'r . . . No, mas'r," kow-towing Tom in Henson. In the novel Uncle Tom died a slave and went to heaven. Not so Henson, at least not until he was 94 and had spent over 50 years in Canada as a free man, famous for the Uncle Tom connection.

name originated when a slave-holder, hot in pursuit of a runaway slave, lost him on the banks of the Ohio River. Furious, he turned to an onlooker and screamed, "The damned Abolitionists must have a Rail-road under the ground by which they run off niggers!" The term stuck.

practical but precarious

The system was run along practical but precarious lines, as Henson discovered. Sympathizers in free states like Ohio and Indiana offered shelter in barns and houses called stations. Slaves were concealed by day, fed and clothed when necessary and then conducted to the next station by a friendly local. They might travel from six to twenty miles in one night. Escapees struggled through the bush on foot with the aid of a compass, the North Star, the thicker moss on the north side of trees, or just by guess. They avoided travelled roads and lit no cooking fires which might attract slave-hunters.

Although Ohio was known as a free state, no slave was entirely safe there because professional trackers constantly sniffed around the country to recover runaways and transport them back to southern plantations. A Fugitive Slave Law, passed by the U.S. Congress in 1850, made any northerner caught harbouring or helping a Black liable to a fine of $1000 and possible imprisonment.

Newspaper advertisements like this one in the Louisianna *Onachita Register* of June 1, 1852, were common:

The undersigned would respectfully inform the citizens of Onachita and adjacent parishes that he is located about two miles and a half east of John White's on the road leading from Monroes to Bastrope and that he has a fine Pack of Dogs for catching Negroes; persons wishing Negroes caught will do well to

give him a call. He can always be found at his stand, when not engaged in hunting; and, even then, information of his where abouts, can always be had of some one on the premises. Terms, 5 dollars per day and found, when no track pointed out; when the track is shown, twenty-five dollars will be charged for catching Negroes.

In his autobiography, Reverend Mitchell recounted watching dogs being trained to hunt blacks on a plantation in North Carolina. Sometimes puppies were given meat or bits of clothing to establish a scent.

Mitchell had been converted to Christianity as a young man and felt guilty for his part in whipping other slaves, including children, when he had been promoted to manage a plantation. After his escape to Ohio, he became deeply involved with the Underground Railroad from 1843 and 1855.

clerical betrayal

One of his first introductions to the Railroad came when a fellow congregationalist and former slave, who had lived freely in Ohio for a number of years, was betrayed by his minister – for $100. Mitchell watched the unfortunate fellow being dragged off with a rope around his neck. He organized a two-hundred-man posse to rescue the man, and from then on his house was a station on the Railroad. In a period of nineteen months, he helped 265 slaves reach Canada and freedom.

Mitchell lived in a number of Ohio communities, one of them close to the Kentucky border where he became "rather notorious as a Negro-stealer." He engineered one runaway's escape by dressing him in a woman's clothes and passing him safely under the noses of slave-trackers. He once witnessed a black mother slit her child's throat when hunters arrived: "It was for your sake I started for Canada," she told her child, "I would

Even the most complex subway map would look simple compared to the "Underground Railroad" network of "stations" stretching from the southern slave states to the Canadian shores of the Detroit River and lakes Erie and Ontario. One fugitive made his way to freedom in a crate marked "This side up with care."

Toronto Blacks twice petitioned city council to ban black-face comedies at saloons and theatres, but in vain. Toronto-born Cool Burgess won international fame for his act.

rather see you dead than go back to slavery."

Few fictional accounts of slavery's horrors outstripped Josiah Henson's story. Born into slavery in Maryland in 1789, Henson had watched while his father's ear was cut off and his back was lashed for knocking down an overseer who had brutally assaulted his wife.

his final run for life

Young Josiah's life was in constant turmoil: he was bought and sold several times, separated from his family and treated unjustly even when loyal. A slave's life consisted of excruciating work from dawn until dusk, and two meals a day (corn-meal and salt-herring with an occasional dollop of vegetables or some buttermilk). Slaves slept, mated, raised children and died in crowded log huts which let in the rain and wind. They slept on planks using their single jackets as pillows. They were issued one pair of shoes each year. Both Henson's shoulders were broken as a result of a tavern brawl in which he rescued his master. He suffered from their improper mending the rest of his life. It was only after a series of hair-raising escapes and recaptures that he made his final run to Canada.

Although freedom was an improvement on slavery, Henson soon realized that the slaves' lack of education and abject attitude led, inevitably, to lack of enterprise. He soon found himself a leader of his people, whom he estimated to number twenty thousand in Upper Canada by the late 1830s.

Establishing a settlement called Dawn near present-day Dresden, Ontario, with other fugitives, Henson wrote:

Several hundreds of coloured persons were in the neighborhood, and in the first joy of their deliverance, they were living in a way, which, I could see led to lit-

96

tle or no progress or improvement. They were content to have the proceeds of their labour at their own command, and had not the ambition for, or the perception of what was within their easy reach, if they did but know it.

His first attempt to improve their lot failed miserably. By pooling resources, Henson and a number of other Blacks purchased land in the area from a certain Mr. McCormick, and began to farm. As it turned out, McCormick hadn't owned the land, and the former slaves found themselves minus their money and still without property. Henson again raised funds and in 1839 managed to purchase two hundred acres of rich land on the Sydenham River, "covered with a heavy growth of black walnut and white wood," for $4 an acre. He urged the establishment of a school for Blacks and the building of a sawmill.

Victoria <u>was</u> amused

During a trip to England to plead the cause of his people and raise funds, Henson exhibited some black walnut from the community farms at the great World's Fair in London. Queen Victoria paid him a call as he stood at his booth, and Henson reported, "I uncovered my head and saluted her as respectfully as I could, and she was pleased with perfect grace to return my salutation."

Henson travelled in the Canadas, Maine, New Hampshire, Vermont, Massachusetts, Connecticut and Rhode Island, speaking in churches and meeting halls to further the cause of abolition. His *The Life of Josiah Henson, formerly a slave, Now an Inhabitant of Canada*, was first published in Boston in 1849.

There is some confusion about whether Harriet Beecher Stowe herself read Henson's book before completing *Uncle Tom's Cabin*. The future bestseller first appeared in serial form in 1851 in a Washington weekly, *The National Era*. It was published in book form in 1852, ten days before the last instalment of the serial appeared, and sold for a dollar.

Henson claimed that Mrs. Stowe sent for him in 1849, when she was living in Andover, Massachusetts, and there he elaborated upon the details of his life. Mrs. Stowe did not publish the fact of their meeting, although she is said to have acknowledged it in a letter to Henson.

the proud prototype

But after the world-wide popularity of *Uncle Tom's Cabin* and the subsequent "Key" in which Mrs. Stowe explained the book and her sources, Henson was referred to as the prototype of Uncle Tom. "I feel proud of the title," Henson said at the time. There is no doubt that he capitalized on Uncle Tom's fame when he conducted his subsequent abolitionist campaigns.

Slaves were always relieved when they reached Canadian soil no matter how difficult the journey, but there were still many problems to be faced. Mitchell, in his book *Underground Railroad*, wrote:

It is a glorious thing to gaze for the first time upon a land, where a poor Slave, flying from a so-called land of liberty, would in a moment find his fetters broken. Even here, it is too true, they find they have only exchanged the yoke of oppression for the galling fetters of a vitiated public opinion.

Sympathy for Black refugees was to be found in many places, but complete acceptance, even in the Canadas, was a myth. Despite the enthusiastic support given to the civil rights cause by such men as George Brown, editor of *The Globe*, Blacks were often the butt of sometimes subtle, sometimes blatant prejudice.

Touring U.S. theatre groups usually included black-face "plantation skits" in their repertoire,

ONE PENNY REWARD.
RAN AWAY from the Subscriber, on *Thursday*, 7th inst., JOHN MENHENNICK, an indented Apprentice to the Blacksmithing Business. This is to caution any person or persons from harboring or employing the said JOHN MENHENNICK, as they will be prosecuted to the utmost rigor of the law.
WILLIAM DAVY.
Kingston, March 8th, 1844.

RUNAWAY APPRENTICE.
THE public are hereby cautioned against hiring, harboring, or otherwise, my apprentice, ROBERT SUTHERLAND, Jun. (who has left my employment, before the expiry of the term of his apprenticeship); as any person so doing will be prosecuted to the utmost rigor of the law.
JAMES POOLE.
Carleton-Place Herald office
August 14th, 1854.

NOTICE.
WHEREAS, THOMAS DONALDS, an Indentured Apprentice, has absented himself from me without any just cause or provocation, I hereby forbid any person or persons from harboring or trusting him on my account, as I will not be responsible for any debts of his contracting; and any person employing him, will be prosecuted according to law.
ROBERT BRASH,
Blacksmith, Portsmouth.
Portsmouth, April 16, 1847.

A strict system of indenture bound servants and apprentices to their employers for contracted periods, during which they were expected to do household work or earn their keep while they learned the trade. Hundreds of notices (like the ones above) in newspapers suggest that many masters abused their help, and probably as many workers were simply good-for-nothing laggards.

According to Alfred Waddinton's account (1858), an "indescribable array of Polish Jews, Italian fishermen, French cooks, jobbers, speculators, land agents, auctioneers, hangers on, bummers, bankrupts and brokers" converged on Victoria after news of the Fraser gold strikes spread. To control this "anti-British element," Governor Douglas organized a militia, with one regiment made up of U.S. refugee Blacks, called the "Sir James Douglas Coloured Regiment" (above).

and such tawdry spectacles were regular fare at both the high-class Theatre Royal and the seedy Apollo Saloon in Toronto. A petition from the city's Blacks in 1840 drew council's attention to the matter, and a licencing by-law prohibited such shows. But well into the 1860's, Blacks continued to be portrayed as "illiterate, barefoot, banjo-strummin' darkies" on the stages of Canada's opera houses.

In some towns racial discrimination barred Black children from attending public schools. Mary Ann Shadd, editor of the *Provincial Freeman* and a tough-minded crusader, singled out St. Catharines, Hamilton and Chatham in her attack on segregation, and throughout the 1850s steered the campaign for racial equality. In Windsor, her editorials were echoed by H.C. Bibb, editor of *The Voice of the Fugitive*, another abolitionist paper.

Meanwhile, the tide of circumstance continued to bring more and more Blacks to Canada. In 1852, the Toronto *Colonist* reported new arrivals with every ship anchoring in the bay. By the end of the decade, of the million people in Canada West, an estimated sixty thousand were Blacks, with an immigration high of twelve hundred in a single year.

a modest majority

Although the majority lived by modest means, after the first good harvests some farmers were able to afford a substantial two-storey frame house, a good barn and small herds of livestock. Those in the towns and cities plied their old trades or learned new skills, sometimes reaping handsome profits from their businesses.

The 1846 *Toronto Directory* lists several dozen Blacks as proprietors: carpenters, shoemakers, drovers, shopkeepers, bricklayers, tailors, waiters and various other tradesmen. Among these, the directory also lists a tobacconist, a physician, two ice vendors, a barber and hairdresser, and two hotel owners.

The tobacconist, Wilson Ruffin Abbott, came to Canada in 1835 from Mobile, Alabama, after his grocery store had been put to the torch. While stocking the humidors and snuff boxes of Toronto's smokers, he dealt on the side in real estate, and was one of the benefactors of the Colored Wesleyan Methodist Church of Toronto when the congregation broke away from the Methodists. (The Blacks refused to support the church's alliance with white pro-slavery southern synods.)

the first Black doctor

In twenty-five years Wilson Abbott was a wealthy man. Among his holdings were forty-two houses and various lots in Toronto, Hamilton and Owen Sound. And what's more, he had paid his son's way through university and medical school. There was probably no prouder father in Canada the day that Anderson Ruffin Abbott received his licence to practice – the first Black doctor in the country.

The two ice vendors, T.F. Carey and R.B. Richards, started their business by cutting and carting ice from the ponds north of Yorkville. A century before refrigerators automatically dropped ice cubes into waiting buckets, the two provided Toronto's fish markets, hotels and homes with crystal-clear, spring-water ice and quickly made a substantial profit. Within years the partnership was operating three ice supply houses, a barber shop on King Street and a bathhouse on Front and Church.

The barber and hairdresser listed in the *Toronto Directory* may well have been the Butlers, who came to the city when it was still called York. Regarded by their wealthy and vain clients as little better than servants, Mrs. Butler must have spent hours combing and curling the tresses of society

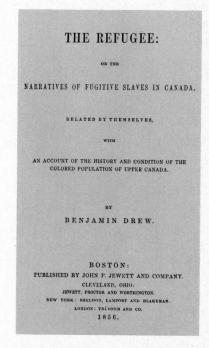

Compiled by Benjamin Drew from his interviews and the written accounts of 117 fugitive slaves in Canada, The Refugee (1856), was published by an abolitionist press in Boston. In its preface, the Anti-Slavery Society of Canada estimated the "coloured population of Upper Canada" at 30,000 in 1852.

**William Hall
The Hero of Lucknow**

The first Canadian to be awarded the coveted Victoria Cross for valour was the Nova Scotia-born son of an ex-slave from Virginia who had escaped to Halifax aboard a British warship during the War of 1812. In 1852, 16-year-old William Hall went to sea with the Royal Navy and saw his first action in the Crimean two years later. When sepoys in the British Army in India mutinied in 1857, laying siege to Lucknow, a naval brigade was sent to relieve the city's garrison. Under heavy fire, William Hall made his way to one of his ship's silenced guns and fired one charge after another until the Indian defences crumbled. Three years later, proudly displaying the Empire's highest military award, he was a crew member on the HMS *Hero* that brought the Prince of Wales to Canada for the first royal tour. He died at 74, at Avonport, N.S.

ladies into the extraordinary bouffant styles of the day. It paid off, though. By the mid-1830s, her tonsorial arts were well known, and the Butlers themselves were wealthy enough to afford, yes, white servants.

respectability's cost

One of the two Black hotel owners, James Mink, ran a highly successful hotel with adjoining stables in the early 1840's. Mink attracted a lively trade, and when he retired had accumulated such a fortune that he could afford to spend $10,000 to find a "respectable" white husband for his daughter. After the wedding, the young couple set out to honeymoon in the southern United States – where the groom sold his bride into slavery. Mink and some Canadian friends paid a large sum of money to bring her back to Toronto.

Another Toronto hotel on the northeast corner of Church and Colborne streets was run by a Black named Snow. The original frame building was replaced by a brick one in 1848, and Snow worked as landord for another four years in partnership with a man called Wright. After a falling-out between them, Snow rented the Epicurean Recess on the east side of Church Street and continued in business for himself.

Blacks were not nearly so successful in the Maritimes. For them it was one long struggle against impossible odds. They had been part of Maritime society before the American Revolution, when some five hundred slaves lived in Nova Scotia. Slaveholding Loyalists brought in a thousand more after the revolution. There were another three thousand Blacks in Nova Scotia freed by the British when they seized American territory during the revolution. Many of these freed slaves served as soldiers or sailors with the English navy and in

various army regiments.

In theory, emancipated Blacks were supposed to receive the same one hundred acres of land as whites but few did, and those who actually received land were given barren lots almost impossible to cultivate. They did not have the resources to begin farming, and government aid was spasmodic at best. Fifteen years after the revolution, many Maritime Blacks were forced to seek jobs as servants just to say alive.

More Blacks escaped to the Maritimes during and after the War of 1812, when the British offered them freedom if they would enlist in the British military. Two thousand arrived in Nova Scotia in 1815 and this time received more aid. However, their land was still poor in comparison with that given to whites. Most Blacks stayed in the Halifax area, where they were allotted small holdings of from eight to ten acres. They were given "licences of occupation" (presumably to protect them from unscrupulous landgrabbers), which meant they could not sell the property. It was twenty-five years before they were given outright ownership of their farms.

goin' home

If Canadian history seems peculiarly devoid of the names of Blacks during the century following the outbreak of America's civil war, it is partly because many thousands of those who sought refuge in Canada for a time returned to the United States. After Lincoln's announcement of the Emancipation Proclamation in 1863, only two thousand remained in Toronto. In fact, Dr. Anderson Ruffin Abbott, a Canadian by birth, himself joined the Union Army as a medic, and was honoured by Abraham Lincoln for his service before he returned to Canada.

100

The 1846 Toronto Directory listed over a hundred Blacks as proprietors of businesses: ice merchants, hair dressers, tailors, hotel keepers, shoemakers, restauranteurs, tobacconists, carpenters, etc. By 1860, when this photo (looking north up Victoria Street) was taken, the city's Blacks numbered 2,000.

Coke Smyth's sketch of the private chapel of the Ursuline Convent in Quebec (first built in 1641, destroyed by fire and rebuilt three times) is a strange puzzle of a picture. While the nuns celebrate Mass in the sanctuary, an Indian woman and child look on from outside two massive doors and a frame.

102

CHAPTER NINE

The Revelations of Maria Monk

A most horrible outrage has again been perpetrated there [Carbonear, Nfld.] upon an individual, whose only offence seems to have been that he was employed in the office of a Protestant newspaper....

"Vandalism in Newfoundland," London *Times,* June 25, 1840

The book was explosive: a tract guaranteed to fertilize existing hatreds between Protestants and Roman Catholics in every province. Thousands of Canadians, eager to brighten their day with fresh scandal, lapped up *The Awful Disclosures of Maria Monk: Being the sinful secrets of life in a convent, and how an innocent young woman was introduced to a life of depravity.*

What was this literary dynamite that sent dangerous ripples through Canadian society for at least fifty years after its publication? According to the author, it was the rivetting revelations of a young and pregnant nun, a converted Protestant who became so corrupted by the priesthood that she finally fled her convent to New York to tell her tale. Since she could neither read nor write, Maria Monk dictated her story to Reverend J.J. Slocum and George Bourne. Even so, she managed to combine a sugary morality with titillating lewdness.

Harper Brothers of New York published it in 1836 and Protestants everywhere soon savoured the *Awful Disclosures* over tea or rum, whispering passages to one another and exchanging tidbits on convent life. Shocking though much of it was, many Protestant stalwarts generously admitted that the book was merely a confirmation of suspicions they had long entertained about papism.

During the 1840s, the Protestant fear of eventual Catholic domination was given a sharp boost by the sudden influx of Irish-Catholics during the great potato famine. Protestants were ready to discredit the Roman Catholic Church at every turn and *The Awful Disclosures* seemed a provident opportunity to do just that.

Maria Monk's juicy list of infamies was comprehensive. Nuns, she reported, took their confirmation vows from the depths of a coffin; were punished for even the smallest indiscretion by the use of leather gags; were ritually ravished by priests and, when necessary, strangled their own babies. A convenient underground passage connected the Hôtel-Dieu Convent with a nearby monastery. An equally handy lime-pit in the convent cellar effectively disposed of unwanted infants.

With reference to priestly visits Maria wrote, "Few imaginations can conceive deeds so abominable as they practiced." (The minds of Protestants, already reeling with details, tried hard to imagine). Due to their dissolute habits, priests required constant treatment for "attacks of

Religious bigotry often flared in 19th century Canada, fanned by salacious books and pamphlets such as The Awful Revelations of Maria Monk *and* The Priest, The Woman and the Confessional, *published (with this cover illustration) by a defrocked French priest named Charles Chiniquy (see page 104).*

The Apostate Apostle

When Charles Chiniquy died at ninety, over 10,000 people filed past his bier: some, ex-followers of the "Jekyll and Hyde" *abbé;* others, new converts of "le Luther du Canada." Born in 1809 in Kamouraska, he became a priest at 24, and as the "Apostle of Temperance" in the 1840s, led thousands to take the pledge. Sexual escapades and charges of arson and embezzlement ended his priesthood but not his "ministry." Embraced by Protestants, he became a renegade minister and waged a war of slander against the Church, publishing trumped-up scandals and exposés.

disease" which was provided by the unwilling nuns. Maria said she watched a bishop and a priest trample a teenage nun to death on a cot. Rape during confession was commonplace. Maria was forced to drink water in which the Mother Superior had washed her feet. Two sad nuns were locked for years in a pitch-black hole and fed once a day through a trap door.

Not only that – nuns of all ages, including one Mother Superior, disappeared with frightening regularity, never to be seen again. As an exotic touch, the convent harboured a silent, motionless nun who wore a pure white habit and spent a few hours each day in a glass cage, the remainder of her time supposedly in heaven.

Both Catholic and Protestant worlds shuddered when the book appeared. A series of counter-charges, denials and affirmations spanned the following year. A rebuttal was offered by champions of the Catholic cause in a short volume with a long title: *Awful Exposure of the Atrocious Plot Formed by Certain Individuals against the Clergy and Nuns of Lower Canada, through the Intervention of Maria Monk.* The 130-page treatise disclaimed that Maria Monk had ever seen the inside of the nunnery, let alone been confirmed there. At this suggestion, petitions sprouted on all sides for permission to inspect the inner sanctums of the Hôtel-Dieu.

After some delay, two impartial Protestant clergymen made a tour and reported that there was no resemblance between Maria's descriptions and the real thing. A storm of controversy persisted until, miraculously, a second "escaped nun" appeared in New York, claiming the preposterous title, Saint Frances Patrick, and confirming everything Maria Monk had said.

Eventually both Saint Frances Patrick and Maria Monk were exposed as frauds, and Maria confessed to her children that she had made her "awful disclosures" for money, but had never been paid by the men who put her up to the writing. Driven by remorse to drunkenness and insanity, she spent her last days in a New York jail. Ironically, her daughter converted to Roman Catholicism, and confessed in her autobiography, *Maria Monk's Daughter*, that her highest ambition was to enter the Hôtel-Dieu Convent in Montreal.

The common folk in these uncertain days had other religious concerns as well, two much more real than alleged goings on at a Montreal nunnery. Newspapers and preachers voiced constant reminders of the question of the Clergy Reserves: the Constitutional Act of 1791 had set aside one seventh of Upper Canada as a special preserve of the Church of England. Protestants of various other denominations waged a long and bitter fight to either gain a share for themselves or have the land converted to secular use. (Catholics were notably quiet on this issue.

The problem was still fermenting in 1837, when Protestant denominations made it amply clear that if the Clergy Reserves were not secularized they must be divvied up. W.M. Harvard, president of the Wesleyan Methodist Church in Canada, writing that year to Egerton Ryerson (a preacher in Kingston at the time and editor of the *Christian Guardian*, official paper of Upper Canada Methodists), said "We might find a slice of the loaf highly helpful for our Parsonage houses, Supernumerary Preachers, and students for the ministry at Cobourg." The issue bubbled above and below the surface until 1854 when the Reserves were secularized.

A second and equally sensitive issue in Canada West was the burgeoning common or public school system. The majority of schools in Canada East were separate, run by the Catholic Church. But in Canada West, over-whelmingly Protestant, separate schools were a thorn in the side of just about everybody. The two provinces shared a single legislature after 1840, and Protestant voters felt

A Moral Thermometer

How did great-grandpa rate on this "breathalyzer" test published by the *Acadian Recorder*? Well, if he had signed the pledge, as hundreds of thousands from St. John's to Sarnia did in the '40s and '50s, and was a card-carrying member of the Sons of Temperance or the Order of Good Templars, he ranked near the top. But if he started the day with a dram of brandy or rum, made straight for the tavern or grog shop after work and staggered home at night, his vices and diseases probably gave him away long before he reached the −70° mark on the scale.

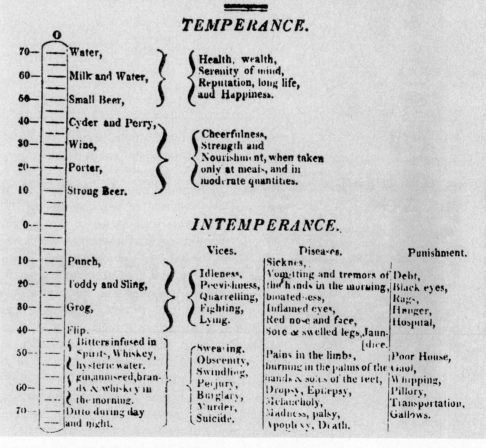

PROGRAMME

OF THE

First Annual Examination of the Model Grammar School

FOR UPPER CANADA, 1859.

WEDNESDAY, the 27th JULY.

CLASSES.	9-9.15, A.M.	9.15-10.	10-10.45.	11-11.45.	11.45-12.30.		1.30-2.15.	2.15-3.	3-3.45.
I.	P R A Y E R S.	English. Mr. STRACHAN.	Modern History and Geography. Rev. Mr. AMBERY.	Ancient Geography. Rev. Mr. AMBERY.	Dictation and Spelling. Mr. STRACHAN.	R E C E S S.		English Grammar. Mr. CHECKLEY.	Arithmetic. Mr. CHECKLEY.
II.		Ancient History. Rev. Mr. AMBERY.	English. Mr. CHECKLEY.	French. Mons. COULON.	Latin. Rev. Mr. AMBERY.		Modern History and Geography. Rev. Mr. AMBERY.		Arithmetic. Mr. CHECKLEY.
III.		Greek. The RECTOR.	Latin Composition. The RECTOR.	Geometry. Mr. CHECKLEY.	Algebra. Mr. CHECKLEY.		Arithmetic. Mr. CHECKLEY.	French. Mons. COULON.	English. Rev. Mr. AMBERY.
IV.		Modern History and Geography. Mr. CHECKLEY.	French. Mons. COULON.	Latin Composition. The RECTOR.	Algebra. Mr. CHECKLEY.		Arithmetic. Mr. CHECKLEY.	English. Rev. Mr. AMBERY.	Greek. The RECTOR.

Even at exam-time, prayers started the day for Upper Canada's grammar (secondary) school students. In the evening of the end-of-the-term ceremony, a model pupil might read her composition, "The Pernicious Effects of Novel Reading."

The Orange Lodges of Canada East and West (with a total membership of 60,000 by 1854) kept the embers of religious hatred glowing through the period, and were behind several murders and head-breakings. Banned by the Secret Societies Bill of 1843, rabid Orangemen burned two of the bill's authors in effigy, and continued their anti-French and anti-Catholic campaign underground.

pressure from eastern Catholic bishops demanding a separate school system in Canada West.

George Brown, influential editor of the *Globe* in Toronto, countered the bishops' demands by proposing the abolition of separate schools. But the politicians were well aware of the growing Catholic vote and decided instead on the School Bill of 1853. Passed in a hurricane of protest, the bill divided public and separate school financing and freed Roman Catholics from paying taxes into the public school fund. Protestants felt their fears of Catholic domination were increasingly justified.

There was yet another vibrant strand in the coarse fabric of mid-nineteenth century life in the Canadas—the Loyal Orange Order. Born in 1688, when Protestant barons swore allegiance to King William III of Orange on England's soil, the pomp and prejudice of the Orange Order was carried to the colonies. The Order was suffocatingly royalist,

stubbornly Tory and staunchly Protestant. At the time of union, there were about twelve thousand Orangemen in Canada West. In their lusty July 12 parades, marching behind a pseudo-King Billy, mounted on a huge white horse, they carried the banner of anti-Catholicism along with their flags.

Violence often broke out. Catholics attacked the Orange Hall in Kingston during the procession of 1843, with some loss of life. The papists were retaliating for a succession of passionate scuffles. The Reform Government attempted to bring in a Secret Societies Act to ban Orange parades. Although the bill died on the floor, its short, bitter struggle for life was instrumental in bringing down the successful Baldwin-LaFontaine coalition. In its place a Party Processions Act scraped through the House, prohibiting King Billys' annual pageant. The act was repealed seven years later, and Orangemen marched once again. Nothing had been

Born in the 1830s, the temperance movement made remarkable headway in all the provinces with rallies and picture-lecture campaigns. In this scene, "the bottle is brought out for the first time," spelling the beginning of the end.

C. & J. MITCHELL,
LOVEJOY HOUSE,
KING STREET, TORONTO.
LIVERY STABLE AND BOWLING SALOON.

At least one inn or tavern marked every major crossroads in colonial Canada, and main "highways" usually supported a dozen or more. In the city of Toronto (population 30,000) there were 152 taverns and 206 beer shops in 1850. After an evening's tippling, drunken brawls and fist-fights were frequently part of the "floor show," and in 1841, during the heated election campaign, one man leaving Allan's Tavern (a hot-bed of fanatical Orangemen) was shot dead from a top-floor window.

gained except a deepened resentment.

Into this slumbering volcano came a vital and dangerous prophet. For people of mid-century Canada, religious meetings were a source of entertainment as well as spiritual solace. Alessandro Gavazzi with his stagey, charismatic style quickly became a messiah.

Gavazzi had been a monk in Italy, but having broken with the Church over the Pope's reactionary attitude during the revolution in Italy in 1848, he was touring North America to raise funds for comrades on the continent. His evangelical zeal endeared him to Protestant hearts. In Canada West he managed to blaze a trail of demonstrations without actually starting any riots, but Canada East was tinder to his sparking oratory.

When Gavazzi preached in Quebec City's Free Presbyterian Church on June 6, 1853, a hostile mob broke into the building and it took the military to tidy up. From then on, the militia insisted on escorting Gavazzi about Montreal for his own safety and to keep the peace.

In Montreal, tempers boiled in the June heat. Irish Roman Catholics, on the hunt for trouble, followed a warm spoor straight to Zion Church where Gavazzi was holding forth to an enthralled audience. The intruders were armed, and in a matter of minutes shots were exchanged. By the time troops had things in hand, ten civilians had been killed in the melee and many others wounded. For days afterwards, Montreal's evangelical churches were battered with stones. The hooligans eventually cooled and fell into uneasy silence, but Gavazzi had added another chapter to the long religious squabble.

The cup of hatred slowly filled and finally overflowed to produce a martyr.

On a clear October day in 1855, at a small

country fair in Canada East, the air curdled with the bitter zest of murder. It was as if all previous outbreaks, all earlier eruptions, inevitably led to this day in St.-Sylvestre. While hundreds of farmers and their wives stood about gawking, trembling and murmuring a few half-hearted protests, Robert Corrigan was battered to death.

He had committed the singular crime of converting from Catholicism to Protestantism. A dozen of his neighbours – Irish, quite ordinary men in most ways, yet obviously fanatics when it came to religion – undertook to deliver his punishment.

The conspirators had not started out to murder him. Their aim, originally, fell short of that. At a meeting held in a barn just before the attack, Richard Kelly, Francis Donaghue, Patrick Donaghue, George Monaghan, Patrick O'Neill, John McCaffrey and George Bannon, along with a handful of others, announced their intention "to mangle and maim" Corrigan.

When the time came, the plot unfolded exactly as planned. First McCaffrey objected to Robert Corrigan's sheep-judging, and when Corrigan bent forward to wipe his hands on a sheep and quit judging, Patrick Donaghue struck him on the head from behind with a big stick. A whistle signalled the others to join in.

According to a witness at the subsequent trial, Corrigan rose with a bloody face while Kelly accused him of having thrown a stone. Corrigan denied it, and Kelly then knocked him down and then jumped up and down on his stomach.

When the assailants finally departed, a bystander suggested that Corrigan be taken to Machell's farm. Corrigan refused saying he was in too much pain. But Kelly, apparently having second thoughts, helped the stricken man to a spot near the Machell house and laid Corrigan against some pine logs. Kelly then disappeared into the house saying that Corrigan "deserved all he got."

The victim was later taken to Andrew McKee's house and given aid.

While the conspirators wined and dined inside the Machell place, Corrigan lay dying. His bowels had burst and he knew the end was not far away. The McKees put him to bed and dressed his wounds, but within hours his abdomen swelled alarmingly and he ran a high fever. "I will never see my poor children," he moaned while a clergyman, a physician and a magistrate prepared for his death. His wife arrived to console him as best she could. Just before he died, he clearly stated, "Kelly is my murderer".

Although the government offered a £100 reward for the arrest of each of the murderers, neither police nor military seemed able, or inclined, to collect. The press, especially in Toronto, was incensed. George Brown's *Globe* enquired "are Protestants to be killed like dogs?" It seemed so.

Four months later, assured by their lawyer that "nothing would come of it," the seven gave themselves up to stand trial.

In the chill of February, 1856, a courtroom in Quebec City – presided over by two Roman Catholic judges and a Roman Catholic jury – was warmed, apparently, by the evidence. There was a great deal of laughter. A clownish veneer spilled over the case culminating in a verdict of "not guilty".

A fresh uproar followed. The *Bowmanville Statesman* queried, "The Pope rules Canada why not St.-Sylvestre?" Most Canadian Protestants believed it to be true and a number of violent incidents followed the Corrigan murder.

When the outcries and protests subsided, the casualties over the years could be counted but the benefits of such strife could not. Gradually the religious violence diminished, and by the time the next decade began, it was, at least to outward appearances, over.

UP WITH THE STANDARD OF TEMPERANCE.

Tune—Up with the Standard of England.

Up with the Standard of Temperance,
Let the watchword alone be ADVANCE;
Up with the Standard of Temperance—
The brave cause we have met to enhance.
CHORUS—Up with the Standard, &c.

Hark! how the tavern-keeper's roaring:
List! list, to the growl of him there;
Far above him pure temperance is soaring,
Its crescent waves high in the air.
CHORUS—Up with the Standard, &c.

'Tis fearful that time should be wasted,
'Tis dreadful that talent should lie dead,
That the horrors of drink should be tasted,
That the Scaffold and Grave should be fed.
CHORUS—Up with the Standard, &c.

When crusaders first raised their "Standard of Temperance," beer and wine were exempted from the list of condemned beverages. When this lax policy failed utterly, complete abstinence became the rule, and anthems like "Sparkling and Bright" and "Cold, Clear Water" were added to the teetotaller's repertoïre.

In new, small communities where all the settlers were of a common faith and background, conflicts were generally smoothed over by the parish priest or minister. Immigrants, like this group of Scottish Presbyterians in Cape Breton, sometimes brought the pastor along with the congregation to the new country.

The Artist of Rue des Jardins

Day-dreaming in front of Notre-Dame Cathedral, the first thing Antoine Plamondon found out in Paris was "the hand is quicker than the eye" – a pickpocket lifted his watch! The 22-year-old artist, a grocer's son, had just finished his apprenticeship in Quebec under Joseph Légaré, and was furthering his studies in Europe. Five years later he was back home, painting the portraits of Quebec's high society: full-face close-ups, stunningly precise in their details of expression and fashion. Before his death at age 91 in 1895, only his student, Théophile Hamel, rivalled his excellence.

Plamondon painted the portraits of Louis-Joseph Papineau and his wife and daughter (above) a year before the Patriot rebellions erupted in 1837.

Teaching drawing at the Hôpital-Général, Plamondon painted three portraits of nuns working there. Soeur Saint-Alphonse (1841) is perhaps his finest.

Around 1850, the restless and irksome artist moved from his studio on the Rue des Jardins to a farm at Neuville, and painted the sons of Alfred Soulard, a local farmer, after their pigeon hunt. The old bachelor's last major work was a self-portrait at age 80.

Nanaimo. The coaling station at Vancouver's Island (1859)

Six years before gold turned the world's attention to British Columbia, the discovery of coal near Nanaimo attracted engineers and miners to Vancouver Island. By 1859, the British Navy had a coaling station at the site (above) and Robert Dunsmuir, a Scottish mine expert, was building his fortune.

CHAPTER TEN

The Emperor's Domain

Two of the men-of-war, the Satellite & Plumper *with ourselves, determined to give a grand ball to the ladies of Vancouver Island. The ladies were very nicely dressed & some danced very well. They would look much better, if they would only learn to wear their crinolines properly.*

Lieutenant Charles W. Wilson, March 15, 1859

Gold. Gold has changed mens' hearts since the first glitter in an Inca God's eye struck a greedy Spaniard's fancy. Gold equals trouble was the watchword of California's Rush of '49 and it was the same again when the first lucky rogues found nuggets along the Fraser River. Dissension and death followed close behind.

When it began, Fort Victoria was a quiet settlement of eight hundred inhabitants, as described by one of the first gold-diggers, Alfred Waddington:

No noise, no bustle, no gamblers, no speculators or interested parties to preach up this or underrate that. A few, quiet, gentlemanly-behaved inhabitants, mostly Scotchmen, secluded as it were from the whole world.

But as rumours of motherlodes spread east and south, the world discovered the quiet outpost and its seclusion ended. Commander Richard C. Mayne of the Royal Navy noted the quickened tempo: "Now, with vessels arriving and leaving constantly, with thousands pouring into the port and 'sensation' news from Fraser daily, a new mind seems to have taken possession of Victoria."

Indeed it had. A tent-city bloomed first and then a sprawl of wooden shacks knocked together by carpenters who might well have been cross-eyed dwarves. Streets were muddy and overrun by cows. Songhee Indians hawked seafood, game and gooseberries. Open sewers ran along the few existing sidewalks. There were no public funds for labour or drain pipes, and drinking water was peddled from horse-drawn carts.

An ethnic segregation set in almost immediately as Jewish merchants and tailors scrambled to set up shop on Johnson Street; Chinese laundries flourished in nearby "little Canton"; Sandwich Islanders (later called Hawaiians) clustered on Kanaka Row (Humboldt Street); the English took to the hills and preserved their formal rituals of tea and ties to the Empire; West Indians and American Negroes rented pews in the city's most fashionable church.

Gold dust wasn't the only source of windfall profit. Real estate values soared from $5 an acre to $500. Speculators promptly divided land and re-sold lots sixty feet by 120 feet for as much as $7,000. Hotels suddenly sprouted, offering third-rate fare at first-rate prices.

Amidst the chaos stood James Douglas – the

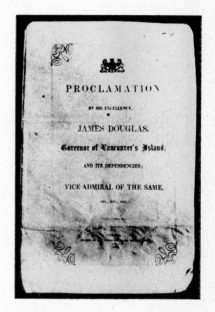

On August 2, 1858, the Hudson's Bay Company's territory of New Caledonia became the crown colony of British Columbia under the governorship of James Douglas, the HBC's *chief factor in the region and Vancouver Island's "emperor."*

113

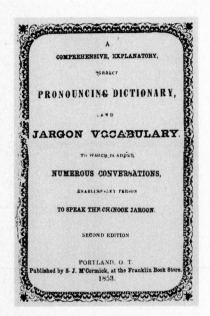

Through their trade with some 40 different Northwest Coast tribes, including the Chinooks, English- and French-speaking Hudson's Bay Company traders created a hybrid language called "Chinook Jargon." In the 1850s, when cartloads of American settlers came pushing and shoving into the Oregon Territory, a Portland printer issued a lexicon of the strange lingo for greenhorns.

only man in the area with the power to back his words. His dominion at the time of the Fraser gold rush stretched from the 49th parallel to the 54th, from the Pacific offshore islands to the mountain ranges of the Great Divide.

Early in Douglas' career, George Simpson, then chief overseas officer of the Hudson's Bay Company described him in a dossier as a "Scotch West Indian." His father had been a successful merchant who educated his son in Lanarkshire, Scotland, but there was considerable confusion around the identity of his mother (who may have been Black) and his birthplace (which may have been British Guiana). At sixteen, Douglas joined the North West Company, a Canadian cartel ferociously fighting the giant HBC for precious beaver pelts. After a brief stay in Fort William at the head of the Great Lakes, Douglas was dispatched to Île-à-la-Crosse, a little outpost two hundred miles northwest of what is now Prince Albert, Saskatchewan.

fusspot accountant

Certain of his characteristics were soon evident. Douglas slaved for the HBC, was a fusspot accountant, had the stamina of Atlas and was an unmitigated windbag. But he was ever-present in time of trouble and brave.

The North West Company and the Hudson's Bay Company merged in 1821 after a long and desperate struggle for control of the vast northern fur-producing region. When Douglas arrived at Fort St. James, an important fur-gathering center in the northern interior of New Caledonia, it was run by Chief Factor William Connolly. Connolly was married in the local fashion to a Cree woman, and eventually Douglas married their daughter. After five years (he was only twenty-seven), Douglas was shifted south to Fort Vancouver, headquarters of the entire western division, situated

near the mouth of the Columbia River. Here he was accountant under Doctor John McLoughlin, a tough autocratic Scot who ruled the HBC's western empire.

McLoughlin ran a tight ship. Fort Vancouver was protected by a twenty-foot stockade enclosing a compound two hundred and fifty by one hundred and fifty yards, housing for employees and white frame residence with a "piazza" for McLoughlin's family. The fort boasted a twenty-four-pound cannon mounted on a ship's carriage and two mortar guns with piles of shot—to impress visitors.

the huge iron rooster

The stillness of the forest was shattered with military regularity by a huge bell. Every morning at exactly five o'clock it wakened the inhabitants like some monstrous iron rooster. Throughout the day it summoned them at precise hours to eat, work, pray and sleep.

Following the same regimented pattern, rations were doled out to each man once a week: eight gallons of potatoes and eight salt salmon, supplemented by peas in the summer. Bread and meat were occasionally added to the fare.

Douglas, like all HBC officers, realized that the days of undisputed rule by the fur-traders in Oregon Territory would soon end. It was likely that the 49th parallel would become the international border west of the mountains. Fort Vancouver and many other Hudson's Bay posts were well below the line. Both Douglas and McLoughlin sniffed about during the 1830's for a safe harbour where they could establish new headquarters when the proper time arrived.

Steering delicate political negotiations had long been a Douglas specialty. When he was still in the northern boondocks, he was dispatched to Sitka, headquarters of the Russian American

The Emperor

In the fur trade fraternity he was known as the "Scotch West Indian"–the son of a sugar plantation owner and a "Creole" woman from British Guiana, where he was born. Schooled in Scotland, 16-year-old James Douglas came to Canada as a North West Company apprentice in 1819. A hot-tempered youth, he was in the thick of skirmishes and duels with the Hudson's Bay men before the 1821 merger ended the fur trade rivalry. By 1826, he was out on the Coast for the HBC, and there he took Amelia, the daughter of Chief Factor William Connolly and an Indian woman, as his wife. Respected by most for his hard work, capable handling of the company's business and his fairness, his heavy-handed rule as the HBC's West Coast "emperor" also made him many enemies, all of whom he outlived or outsmarted. Governor of both Vancouver Island and inland B.C., he established the first farms, sawmills, coal mines, fisheries, roads (including the Cariboo Trail) and towns on the Pacific.

Wife Amelia–"quiet, gentle, simple."

Cecilia–one of Douglas' 13 children.

James Douglas–imperious, penny-pinching, obsessed by details, power and ritual.

"White-headed Eagle" Dr. John McLoughlin left the HBC when the U.S. border was drawn. A "traitor" in Britain, the "Father of Oregon" was left penniless by American land-grabbers.

Company, to meet with officers and iron out differences.

"I held a daily conference with the Governor in a frank and open manner," Douglas reported, "so as to dissipate all semblance of reserve and establish our intercourse on a basis of mutual confidence." In true Douglas style, he never used one word where five would do.

drowned tenure

Just as Douglas and the HBC directors had foreseen, the Oregon border question flooded the Columbia Basin, drowning any possible pleas of tenure by the company. McLoughlin and Douglas were forced to acknowledge "Articles of Compact" with a provisional government of American settlers in 1845. In June, 1846, the Oregon Treaty confirmed what everyone suspected: the 49th parallel was the border on the mainland.

Fortunately, Douglas had earlier selected probable sites for new headquarters by visiting Vancouver Island in 1842 and 1843. The harbour at "Is-Whoy-Malth" (Esquimalt) was deep and sheltered but the area was too rugged for farming. On the other hand, across the water lay Camosun Inlet, with a shallower draw for ocean vessels but clear land, excellent drainage, plentiful timber and acres of natural clover for pasture. He chose the latter and left a junior officer, Charles Ross, in charge of building the fort.

By the time the Oregon Treaty was signed, McLoughlin had retired leaving Douglas as chief agent of an empire which each year shipped half a million dollars in fur to the London market. With Fort Victoria a snug reality well above the new American border, Douglas could shift his headquarters with impunity in 1849.

Large tracts of land were being worked, a sawmill operated successfully and three large dairies had been built. Douglas had nine years to oversee the community before the full force of the gold rush struck. He established schools, a hospital, churches, a little law and order, and ordered surveys of the mainland. Douglas also instructed an employee, Alexander Anderson, to find a safe route from the interior to the navigable waters of the lower Fraser.

Meanwhile, in the slow-grinding mills of the British government, a temporary setback was in store for Chief Agent Douglas. One cold spring morning in 1850, HMS *Driver* appeared in Fort Victoria's harbour bearing the first governor of the crown colony of Vancouver Island, His Excellency Richard Blanshard, Esq. Douglas, who had coveted the appointment himself, ground his teeth and settled in for a long winter. On paper he charitably described the younger man as "gentlemanly" and "prepossessing," but there is no doubt that he regarded the governor as an ignorant nuisance.

Douglas triumphant

For his part, Blanshard had grand intentions but no military support, no personal fortune (he had fully expected to be granted a thousand-acre estate) and no funding from London. He struggled hard to hold the few scraps of power his position warranted, but it was like pitting Tom Thumb against John Bull. Within a year, Blanshard sailed for home and Douglas was governor of the island. He remained chief agent of the company, of course, a conflict of interests which threaded through many of his decisions.

Although gold had been found on the Queen Charlotte Islands in 1850, and traces appeared regularly in the Fraser Valley, Governor Douglas did not become too uneasy until March, 1858. It was after a dozen prospectors camped on a well-established sandbar ten miles upriver from Fort Hope on the Fraser, that a man called Hill first spotted

"WHAT? YOU YOUNG YANKEE-NOODLE, STRIKE YOUR OWN FATHER!".

U.S. president James Knox Polk (the "Yankee Noodle" of this British cartoon) sabre-rattled through the Oregon Boundary settlement talks with his threatening slogan, "54° 40' or fight!"

**Richard Blanshard
Governor Without a Colony**

Even eight months on the job was too long for Vancouver Island's unhappy first governor. Nervous at American expansion in the Pacific Northwest, London decided to anchor its claim and dispatched Richard Blanshard, a 32-year-old barrister, to the post. Eager for experience that might lead to a higher colonial appointment, he accepted the job without initial pay. Blanshard arrived in March of 1850, only to find he had no house to live in and only one permanent colonist. The island was effectively run by James Douglas, the imposing HBC factor who envied Blanshard's title and usurped his authority at every turn. In short, the governor had nothing to govern. High prices at the HBC store were ruining him, and the Colonial Office turned a deaf ear to his grievances. With still no pay, he resigned in November and in the spring paid his own passage home.

"Something between a Dutch toy and a Chinese pagoda" was how Amor De Cosmos of the British Colonist *described Victoria's new Colonial Office building, built in 1859. His rival paper, the* Gazette *called the style "Elizabethan."*

the hypnotic sparkle in moss beneath his feet. Dipping his pan in the water, he quickly washed out a sizeable poke.

Some say over two million dollars worth was panned off Hill's Bar by the end of the year, while others filtered out some of the duller nuggets and diluted the lode to half a million.

Whatever the real take (most miners averaged $8 to $13 a day at the height of the rush), the dazzling news spread to California where a perennial flock of professional buzzards seemingly nested in wait for the latest strike. Within weeks, on every sandbar (large islands formed by the swift but meandering Fraser), shaggy rascals crouched eagerly over rough cradles, pans and sluices, sorting gold from gravel.

Despite the influx of whites, it was still Indian country. There was no organized government. Even territorial rights were in some doubt, though

Queen Victoria had renamed New Caledonia "British Columbia" on August 2, 1858, and established it as a crown colony. But with thousands of Americans squatting, a dyed-in-the-fur-monarchist like Governor Douglas felt compelled to issue rafts of proclamations claiming control of the territory.

The only immutable law in three million square miles was the Hudson's Bay Company's exclusive right to trade with the natives. Douglas, still wearing two hats as late as August, had long been on shaky legal ground. His edicts swung from threats to prosecute miners with no licence to dig (December, 1857), increasing licence fees from eleven to twenty-one shillings per month payable in advance for each digger (January, 1858), to attempting to force an American steamship company to carry only HBC supplies into Fort Victoria and the mouth of the Fraser River (May, 1858).

The only casualty of the "Pig War" between Britain and the U.S. was a stray sow, shot by an American settler on San Juan Island in 1859. British (above) and American troops occupied the island 12 years before the affair was resolved.

**John Sebastian Helmcken
Doctor in the House**

His motives might well be questioned, considering his position as grand panjandrum of the fur and mercantile trade, but he was sincerely attached to the Crown and recalled only too well how Oregon had been swept out of British hands by the steady stream of American settlers. The same fate might easily befall New Caledonia if firm steps were not taken.

As the waves of Americans, Englishmen, Irishmen, Scotsmen and Chinese rolled ever higher up the Fraser River, the situation grew more and more tense. Most immigrants (estimates for the year vary from ten thousand to thirty thousand) boated to Fort Victoria, where they picked up supplies (at inflated prices), purchased a licence to dig and hired a small craft to take them to the mouth of the Fraser. A small army marched from California through Oregon and Washington to the Columbia River and then up the Okanagan Valley as far as Kamloops. They then canoed and portaged across country to the upper Fraser.

Whichever route they chose, they quickly set up camp and unpacked pans. Soon every sandbar on the river sprouted a mushroom of tents and at least one crude saloon made of green logs. Shadowing the miners were unscrupulous merchants, prostitutes, parasites and increasingly hostile Indians.

Prior to the invasion the local Indians had been fairly docile. Traders from the HBC had dealt with these people for twenty years without much difficulty. But now white men were making off with their gold, pilfering their fishing grounds and ravishing their women.

Ominous news filtered north from the new state of Washington, that Indians there were engaged in bloody battle with encroaching white settlers. Hearing this, Indians in the Fraser Valley be-

As he stepped off the boat in 1850 in Victoria, the 26-year-old English doctor's luggage – "lots of seed and canaries" – must have startled a few colonists, but it was obvious that John Helmcken was here to stay. Two years later, well-established in his practice, he married Governor James Douglas' daughter, Cecilia. With 400 adults and their families to attend to, the good doctor at first had some time for gardening, but in 1855, when the colony's first House of Assembly met, he was named Speaker – a post he held until B.C.'s union with Canada in 1871. Advisor (and son-in-law) to the governor, it was natural for Helmcken to rally support for most of Douglas' plans, but he was much more than a "rubber stamp." In 1870, he headed B.C.'s delegation to Ottawa and masterminded the idea of a railway to the Coast as a key condition to Confederation.

119

Victoria, as seen by the city's second photographer, Richard Maynard, was described by the Gazette *in 1859 as a town of "nobs, snobs and flunkies."*
In the heady gold-rush days of 1858, 223 buildings went up around Wharf Street (above), most of them stores run by Americans from San Francisco.

120

came more bold. At first they merely pulled up miners' stakes and stole supplies, but as tension grew they began to scalp and kill.

Once peaceful Fort Victoria had changed; so too had the solemn forests of British Columbia's interior. On the gold fields, both food and dry goods were scarce and costly. Flour fetched $100 a barrel, pork $1 a pound, tea $4 a pound and sugar $2 a pound. Nails were priced at a shilling each. So critical was the food problem (bear meat became boring) that one educated Englishmen, Kinahan Cornwallis, ranging the sandbars as much for pleasure as treasure, reported he and his fellow gold-diggers pitched in to pay a French cook $10 a day. The chef produced "bear a-la-mode, a grill of ditto with grasshopper sauce, prairie greens and yam potatoes and a pudding stuffed with wild raspberries."

guns under pillows

A man wasn't really safe in the gold fields. One black-bearded individual toted two guns at his belt because, as he told Cornwallis, "I guess, I calculate pretty correctly when I say that I've realized three hundred and seventy-three dollars and fifty-eight cents this ar week." Cornwallis himself slept with a gun under his pillow.

One dark night when he had bedded down in a tent where the cook slept amid the pots, crockery and food, a tall Indian burst in. The cook became so excited he "upset a mustard pot over his whiskers in a sudden endeavor to attain the perpendicular." The same unfortunate had no more luck when he tried to go back to sleep, for he "dropped flat on a gridiron when he proceeded to resume the horizontal."

The Indians continued to harass and kill the invaders when they could. Their anger finally exploded in a gruesome affair at China Bar. Fifteen miners were decapitated and their bodies tossed into the rushing waters of the Fraser. Edward Stout and four others managed to retreat to a cave where they were pinned down by rifle fire.

They were rescued by the arrival of H.M. Snyder and about a hundred and fifty miners from Fort Yale, twenty miles down river; vigilantes united against the "murderous aboriginies."

no guns or Chinese . . .

The makeshift militia banished all Chinese from the area for a month in the misguided belief that they had somehow supplied the Indians with rifles and ammunition. Captain Snyder, as the miners called him, then negotiated peace with the local chiefs and the emergency was tempered considerably. It was not long before James Douglas arrived backed by a party of armed men. His visits to the trouble spots restored a semblance of order to the Fraser Valley.

Late in August, when he became governor of both colonies, Douglas reluctantly relinquished his old connections with the Hudson's Bay Company and devoted himself to full-time service to his Queen. By the end of 1858, his efforts were rewarded in part with a knighthood. While Douglas was single-minded, arrogant and often acted without proper authority, through his efforts the destiny of the Pacific Coast was transformed from a mere extension of the American appetite to a gleaming jewel in Victoria's Crown.

Robert Dunsmuir
The Millionaire Coal-Master

There were no unions in 1851, when Robert Dunsmuir came to Victoria. Born in Scotland in 1825, his great-grandfather, grandfather and father had been wealthy coal-masters, and young Robert was simply following in their footsteps. Working first for the HBC developing the fields at Nanaimo, he picked up land along the vein at bargain prices, brought in Chinese labourers, and in no time built a fortune from Wellington Mines. He was just beginning. With good connections in politics and occasional strike-breaking help from the militia, he piled million on million from collieries, iron works, steamships and the Esquimalt and Nanaimo Railway. And what was wrong with that? According to him the working man's best friend was the capitalist-employer! Typical of the "Andrew Carnegies" of his time, Craigdarroch Castle is his epitaph.

Family Portrait

Old family portraits in dusty attic trunks tell remarkable tales, and in many ways, the two family photographs here tell of Canada's transition from its pioneer days to the age of industry. Opposite, a portly Samuel Strickland poses with family and relatives in front of his rambling, stone house in Lakefield, Canada West. Thirty years before, a log cabin occupied the spot. Below, Casimir Gzowski, his wife and seven children congregate on the verandah of their Toronto home in 1855. A Polish engineer, he made his fortune building the Grand Trunk Railway from Toronto to Sarnia.

Born in St. Petersburg, Russia, the son of a Polish count in the Imperial Army, Casimir Gzowski was captured and exiled during the 1830 Polish rebellion. He came to Canada in 1841, and worked as a government engineer before setting up his own firm. Besides railways, he built Niagara's International Bridge.

Brother of Susanna Moodie (Roughing it in the Bush) *and Catharine Parr Traill* (The Backwoods of Canada), *Colonel Sam Strickland (standing, right) published* his *own pioneer memoirs,* Twenty-seven Years in Canada West, *in 1853, a few years before this photo. (Mrs. Traill is third from left, holding a child.)*

Acknowledgements

To find unusual, lively and accurate social history, a writer must read so many books and delve into so many documents that to acknowledge each one becomes impossible. Certain historians are, of course, indispensable: J.M.S. Careless, O.D. Skelton, W.L. Morton among them.

However, I am particularly grateful to the few brave souls who kept meticulous journals through the trials of life in mid-century British North America. I am thinking of people like Robert Whyte and Stephen De Vere (Irish emigrants during the typhus epidemic of 1847), Sophia MacNab, young daughter of Allan Napier MacNab (who offered in her diary a daily account of life in Dundurn Castle), and the wonderful journals of John Franklin, Robert McClure and Francis McClintock, of their polar expeditions.

I'm delighted to have found new heroes like Jane Franklin, who was determined to establish that her husband had found the Northwest Passage; John Palliser, who charted the West; and Paul Kane, who recorded the life of the Plains and West Coast Indians. That they could be so courageous, dashing and far-sighted under stress renews hope for frailer humans like myself.

Finally, a word of thanks to my indomitable researcher, Joan Coleman, who so painstakingly unearthed many rich sources in Canadian history.

Joy Carroll

Photo: Hans-Ulrich Lichtenberg

The Author

Joy Carroll grew up in Melfort, Saskatchewan, and began her professional writing career as a reporter on the Prince Albert *Daily Herald.* She has been a music teacher, church organist, wife, mother of four, CBC typist, radio script writer, an editor for Harlequin Books, and has produced dozens of articles for *Maclean's, Financial Post, Weekend, Canadian Art* and *Seventeen.* She was travel editor for *Chatelaine* for two years and still writes travel articles for several publications. As a novelist she has written over ten books, among them *Proud Blood,* a generational saga set in Montreal at the turn of the century.

Index

The page numbers in italics refer to illustrations and captions

Picture Credits

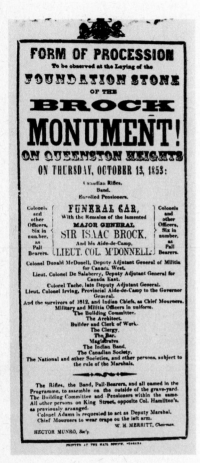

On April 17, 1840 – a not-so-good Good Friday – an Irish-Canadian fanatic named Benjamin Lett, who had fought with the insurgents in the 1837 rebellion and was living in exile in the U.S., slipped into Canada and blew up the Brock monument at Queenston Heights. After the public's outrage died down, a new column was raised with great fanfare to the "Hero of U.C."

We would like to acknowledge the help and co-operation of the directors and staff of the various public institutions and the private firms and individuals who made available paintings, posters, mementoes, collections and albums as well as photographs, and gave us permission to reproduce them. Every effort has been made to identify and credit appropriately the sources of all illustrations used in this book. Any further information will be appreciated and acknowledged in subsequent editions.

The illustrations are listed in the order of their appearances on the page, left to right, top to bottom. Principal sources are credited under their abbreviations:

PAC	Public Archives of Canada
ROM	Royal Ontario Museum
GA	Glenbow-Alberta Institute
MTL	Metropolitan Toronto Library
NGC	National Gallery of Canada
WCC-NBM	Webster Canadiana Collection, New Brunswick Museum
PC	Private Collection
PABC	Provincial Archives, Victoria, B.C.

1 MTL /2 NGC /4 McCord Museum, Montreal /6 MTL /7 MTL /8 MTL /9 PAC C92203 /10 PAC C416533 /11 ROM /12 PAC C80319 /13 Archives Nationales du Québec /14 PAC C11478 /15 Bonscours Church, Montreal /16 WCC-NBM /17 WCC-NBM /18 PC /19 Notman Photographic Archives /20 PC /21 NCG /22 PAC C1425 /23 PC /24 Art Gallery of Ontario /25 PAC /26 PAC C92201 /27 Archives Nationales du Québec /28 PC /29 ROM /30 PAC C92205 /31 PAC C92198 /32 MTL /33 MTL /34 Montreal Museum of Fine Arts; PAC /35 ROM /36 National Portrait Gallery, London /37 MTL /38 ROM /39 PAC /40 MTL /41 MTL; WCC-NBM /42 MTL; PAC C41305 /43 ROM; MTL /44 PAC C4366 /45 GA /46 ROM; ROM /47 ROM /48 PAC /49 MTL /50 Archives Nationales du Québec /51 NGC /52 PAC C2394 /53 PAC /54 Smithsonian Office of Anthropology /55 PAC C13400 /56 MTL /57 NGC /58 PAC C2409 /59 Dalhousie University Library /60 WCC-NBM /61 Public Archives of Prince Edward Island /62 GA; WCC-NBM /63 ROM; MTL /64 Public Archives of Nova Scotia /65 PAC /66 PAC /67 PAC /68 NGC /69 MTL /70 PAC /71 Ralph Greenhill Collection, Miller Services /72 MTL; ROM /73 ROM; CN Archives /74 Ralph Greenhill Collection, Miller Services /75 MTL /76 Archives Nationales du Québec /77 MTL; PC /78 MTL /79 PAC /80 Royal Geographical Society, London /81 MTL /82 PAC C82974 /83 PAC C23580 /84 PABC; PAC C2820 /85 PAC C17034; Hudson's Bay Company /86 MTL /87 PAC C4572 /88 WCC-NBM /89 Special Collection, Dalhousie University Library /90 PAC C17936 /91 PAC /92 Upper Canada Village /93 New York Historical Society /94 MTL /95 Cincinnati Art Museum /96 MTL /97 MTL /98 PABC /99 MTL /100 PAC C18743 /101 MTL /102 PAC C1022 /103 MTL /104 Archives Nationales du Québec /105 Public Archives of Nova Scotia /106 PC; Ontario Archives /107 Vancouver Public Library; MTL /108 Ontario Archives /109 PAC C6886 /110 NGC; NGC /111 Art Gallery of Ontario /112 PAC /113 PABC /114 Oregon Historical Society /115 PABC; PABC /116 PABC /117 PAC /118 PABC; PABC /119 PABC; PABC /120 PABC /121 PABC /122 Ontario Archives /123 PAC PA45005 /128 MTL

1850

Coal discovered on Vancouver Island.

THE GOVERNMENT THIMBLERIG.

Canadian parliament moved to Toronto.

First shipment of B.C. lumber exported to San Francisco.

Fugitive Slave Law in U.S. increases Black immigration to Canada.

1851

First Y.M.C.A. in North America founded in Montreal.

Prince Edward Island granted responsible government.

First Canadian postage stamp designed by Sandford Fleming issued.

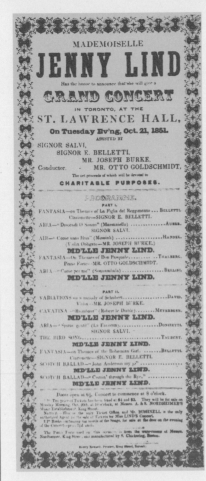

Jenny Lind, "The Swedish Nightingale," packs Toronto's new St. Lawrence Hall on concert tour.

Quebec City becomes capital of Canada.

Grand Trunk Railway Company formed.

The *Marco Polo,* later known as the world's fastest sailing ship, launched in Saint John, N.B.

1852

Toronto tailors strike protesting advent of Singer sewing machine.

Frederick Gisborne lays first North American undersea telegraph cable between New Brunswick and P.E.I.

Susanna Moodie publishes *Roughing It in The Bush.*

Le Séminaire de Québec becomes Laval University.

Fire destroys commercial quarter of Montreal: $1 million damage.

Father Albert Lacombe crosses prairies from St. Boniface to Edmonton House.

First school opens on Vancouver Island.

Rotary printing press invented.

Trinity College opens in Toronto.

Daniel and Hart Massey produce their mowing machine in Newcastle, C.W.

1853

Violence erupts between Protestants and Catholics in Quebec incited by sermon of ex-monk Alessandro Gavazzi.

First ocean steamer arrives at Quebec City.

M'Clure and Belcher expeditions from west and east meet completing Northwest Passage.

Egerton Ryerson appointed chief superintendent of education for Canada West.

Grand Trunk Railway between Montreal and Portland, Maine, completed.

1854

Reciprocity treaty with U.S. opens markets for Canadian products.

Seigneurial system of land tenure abolished in Canada East.

Construction begins on railway from Halifax to Truro, N.S.

St. Francis Xavier College founded at Antigonish, N.S.

Clergy Reserves Act opens church lands for settlement.

Octave Cremazie, Quebec bookseller and first major poet, publishes first work.

1855

Newfoudland granted responsible government.

Hudson's Bay Company signs treaty with Alberta Blackfoot Nation.

Henry Walters builds axe factory in Aylmer, Quebec, which becomes largest in Empire.